A Wonderful Spiritual Journey

by
Alan Seymour

To my dear friends
Mollie and Peter

It's been a wonderful
journey with you by
my side

Alan
xx

Published in 2014 by FeedARead.com Publishing

Copyright © Alan Seymour.

First Edition

A CIP catalogue record for this title is available from the British Library.

Published in 2014 by FeedARead.com Publishing

Contents

Acknowledgements

I wish to thank everyone who has helped me with this journey, especially Mollie and Peter McManus without whom the journey would not have begun and progress would not have been possible.

Pat Deverell, who passed to Spirit in October 2008, and gave me much encouragement during a difficult time in my life, helped me to enhance my mediumship and trance work and I am sure she has been inspiring me from the world of Spirit since her passing.

Last, but not least, my lovely wife Pat, who has supported and encouraged me in so many ways, through our church, through the Spiritualist religion and in the production of this book, helping to transcribe hours of recordings from the trance demonstrations, while dedicating her time to make her own progress in our religion.

Foreward

When I decided to start a home circle in 1991 I never expected that it would lead to the wonderful, interesting and enlightening pathway that opened up to myself and particularly Alan Seymour.

Looking back with the knowledge of the Spirit world I now have, after 24 years, I realise that it was all arranged by those in the Spirit world, and today that does not surprise me, as I am very aware of their influence in our lives and how determined they can be.

Our intention was to just improve our development as we felt that sitting one evening a week in the church circle was not sufficient and we should give more time to something so important to us.

We just wanted to improve our link with Spirit, but it was not long before one of our members showed signs of going into a trance state leading to our circle became a trance circle, starting our wonderful journey with those in the Spirit world.

In this book you will see where that journey took us over the years to where we are now.

I strongly believe that we were led all the way and I am so pleased that we have recordings and written transcripts to refer to which authenticate all the fantastic sittings that we experienced.

It is obvious to me now that the whole object of the circle was for Alan to develop as a trance medium in order that his Spirit guide, Fine Feather should eventually be able to speak in public, bringing his knowledge and wisdom to us all.

Another side to Alan's trance mediumship has been to help those poor souls who have been unable or perhaps unwilling, to complete their journey to the other side.

We can only do this work with the knowledge that our friend Fine Feather is always in the background to protect us and step in if needed.

I have had many conversations with Fine Feather over the years and he has become a close friend to me. So much so that occasionally I have disagreed with him when it comes to modern earthly matters which he doesn't always understand.

I know that those who attend one of Alan's trance demonstrations for the first time find my greeting of Fine Feather and our friendly conversations rather odd, but as far as I am concerned it is not Alan sitting in the chair beside me but my friend of nearly twenty five years, Fine Feather.

We have doubted at times, some of the things that Fine Feather has foretold, but over the years they have happened, although at the time they seemed unlikely.

I am now in my 17th year as President of Croydon National Spiritualist Church and Alan has been Vice President for the same period of time. A situation that Fine Feather predicted years before, saying that we would become 'leading lights' in the Church. Just one of the things that we doubted at the time.

If by setting up my home circle all those years ago I was the instigator of Alan's relationship with Fine Feather, we must be truly grateful for it has brought us much insight into the Spirit world and a great deal of pleasure.

I wish to thank Alan for all his hard work in putting this book together and to thank him and his wife Pat for their friendship and support. I could not have achieved what I have without them.

I hope you will enjoy our journey with the Spirit world and especially with our friend, Fine Feather.

Mollie McManus OSNU LSSNU

Preface

There is a growing understanding in the United Kingdom and many other parts of the world that the death of physical body is not the end of our lives.

More and more people are accepting that our physical existence is merely a 'school' and that during our time here we learn lessons, experience good and bad, love and hatred, compassion and selfishness. At the point of death we merely shed our aging or diseased bodies while our Spirit or Soul, containing memories of all our experiences, continues to exist in the world of Spirit.

The personality remains intact in the Spirit world and continues to grow, gaining more knowledge throughout its existence into the eternal light of God.

With this knowledge, many people are questioning the orthodox view that it is somehow wrong to communicate with those loved ones who have passed to Spirit and are consulting mediums who are often able to allow a dear departed loved one to communicate their continued existence in another dimension we call the Spirit world.

Even believers in orthodox religions tend to accept life after death.

This is confirmed when we look around greeting card shops selling cards of bereavement which show many such cards giving words of comfort that speak of someone being 'in the next room' or 'still watching over you' even though they are physically 'dead'.

A medium's evidence can take the form of a description of the communicator, perhaps his age, name, profession, cause of death, along with the communicators awareness of events taking place in the sitters life that cannot be known by anyone but the sitter or his family.

Thus, the evidence given will cause the sitter to seek further information and perhaps visit his nearest Spiritualist church in an effort to understand more about the philosophy and history of the Spiritualist religion (the 7th most popular religion in the United Kingdom).

The individual will then become aware of so much more that the religion can offer, including Spiritual healing, a non-dogmatic approach to religion along with other forms of mediumship including physical phenomena and trance communication.

Trance mediumship is an important method of proving life after death and is relatively rare in the religion of Spiritualism.

When I say 'rare' I don't imply that there are very few trance mediums, but that there are relatively few who have developed the ability to trust Spirit enough to allow someone in the Spirit world to use their bodies, minds and voice box, to reveal themselves in a physical way in a public demonstration.

Trance mediumship is different from mental mediumship in the sense that a demonstration of mental mediumship requires clairaudience (clear hearing), clairsentience (clear sensing) or clairvoyance (clear seeing).

The medium then interprets what he is hearing, sensing or seeing to pass on a verbal message to a recipient.

Trance mediumship requires the use of the mediums physical body.

Because Spirits no longer have physical bodies it is necessary for them to make use of individuals who have developed themselves sufficiently as mediums, to express their own personalities through the body and consciousness of the medium, and thus, communicate to the audience using the medium's voice box.

To enable this to happen, the medium has to learn to relax his mind and make himself less aware of his own thoughts, feelings and surroundings.

As he does this, he is opening himself up to the influence of people living in the Spirit world who wish to communicate through the medium.

Evidence that there is a discarnate Spirit speaking usually takes the form of a complete change of voice and personality, along with a depth of knowledge that the medium is known not to have.

Sometimes the discarnate Spirit may be known to a member of the audience who will verify the information given to be accurate, while recognising the individual through the physical characteristics shown, the tone of voice and the way of speaking.

It is the purpose of this book to show that trance mediumship is a wonderful form of mediumship and within its pages, the reader will learn that, through dedication and patience by people living on both sides of the 'veil' that separates the two worlds, communication is possible and that by allowing people to communicate, we can learn a little more about the purpose of our physical lives and how we can all work together to make the world a better place in which to live.

Introduction

When I began writing this book it was to bring to a greater number of people the wonderful communications received from my guide, Fine Feather, a man of such stature and with such a presence that it is a humbling experience to know him.

It is suggested that we each have a guide in the Spirit world who is with us from the day we are born, helping us inspirationally throughout our physical lives and being able to respond to our needs, if only we would ask.

The book charts the progress of the development circle started at the home of my good friends, Mollie and Peter McManus whom I met when I started attending the mediumship development circle at Croydon Spiritualist Church in 1987.

I had been invited to join the Church circle by the then Vice President of the church, Pat Robertson. Never having attended such a group before, I was very nervous and hesitant about what to expect.

The purpose of the church development circle was to enable individuals to realise their own potential in making their own connection with the people living in the Spirit world.

This is generally achieved, initially, by meditation and learning to become less aware of our physical surroundings and slowly allowing the subconscious mind to come to the fore. It is during this time of peacefulness that new experiences are allowed to progressively reveal themselves in the form of light, colour and misty shapes until eventually the 'trainee' becomes more trusting in the fact that there is some form of intelligence behind these manifestations.

After a number of years I gradually became more self confident and able to practice working on the church platform, firstly giving a reading on the philosophy of Spiritualism to the congregation during services from books such as the Silver Birch teachings, progressing to attempting an address, followed by my first tentative efforts to give a message from a person in the Spirit world to a member of the circle.

My very earliest memory of having given a semi-trance address from the church platform was during one of these circle evenings when I was asked to get onto the platform and attempt to give a talk about Spiritualism.

I had no recollection of what I had said but remember being praised by members of the circle after I had finished.

With hindsight I believe that I must have been entranced or at least inspired by an individual in the Spirit world to speak, because the praise I received was not typical of that given after my previous efforts at speaking, as I had been very nervous of attempting any form of public speaking.

After about four years, it was becoming obvious that our curiosity about Spiritualism was not being satisfied by the fairly slow progress of the church circle and although many of us were now regularly speaking and demonstrating mediumship in the circle and indeed at church services, Mollie asked a few of us if we would like to join her in setting up a regular circle in her home 'just to see what might happen'.

We had no preconceived ideas as to what we were sitting for. Improvements in our mediumship perhaps, physical phenomena, involving the movement of objects or hearing sounds caused by activity from 'unseen forces' (surely far too ambitious!).

Perhaps even, trance. Nevertheless, we sat regularly, eager to learn, in the hope that our commitment might bring results, in the knowledge that the many pioneers of Spiritualism sat for months, sometimes years, before their dedication produced any contact with the Spirit world.

What follows in this book is the story of our progress. From sitting weekly for two hours when nothing much appeared to be happening, to the gradual awareness of people residing in the Spirit world who wished to communicate with us.

Nothing could have prepared us for the wonderful journey on which we were about to embark.

Early Progress

In the summer of 1991 Mollie McManus asked if we might begin to sit in a development circle at her home 'just to see what might occur'. The circle consisted of Mollie, her husband Peter, myself and fellow church member, Melvin Steer.

Initially very little happened, but by October there were indications that Melvin and I had somebody with us who wished to speak.

Melvin soon became aware of someone wishing to communicate and with prompting from Mollie, a man calling himself Joseph began to speak. He said that he had lived in America, was a French Canadian, working and living at a trading post in about 1740.

Joseph revealed that he was Melvin's healing guide, and that he had with him a friend named Michaël, who was trying to communicate through Alan but was having problems because Alan was not relaxed enough to allow him to speak and partly because Michaël appeared to be shy.

After a while Michaël was able to say 'hello' but little else, however Joseph continued to speak through Melvin each week, stating that he and Michaël had lived in Saskatchewan, Canada in a homestead in a valley at the foot of the mountains.

He stated that they were 'Christos', which when Mollie asked for the meaning of the word it became clear that they were Christians.

They had spoken French but had learned some English from a preacher named David during their time at Saskatchewan.

Mollie suggested that language was not a problem in the Spirit world as communication was a thought process, and Joseph agreed.

Gradually, Michaël began to speak and revealed that he was shy because he'd had a speech impediment, (Alan felt that it was a deformity of Michaël's mouth); however a conversation began between Joseph and Michaël, during which they reminisced about their time in Saskatchewan.

They remembered dancing twice a year in a barn in a harvested field.

Michaël was asked if he had married and had children, to which he replied that he had. He was the father of three girls.

Joseph was asked if he had married and he said that he had not.

Michaël's progress continued until he managed to speak more clearly. We felt that this was because, through illness, Melvin was unable to attend regularly and therefore Joseph was unable to communicate without him.

Peter asked Michaël questions about the outpost he and Joseph had lived in and Michaël said that the house he lived in was very small and by a lake and life was very hard.

They lived among the Indians which could be difficult at times due to mistrust and sometimes outbreaks of violence. Nevertheless they gradually learned from one another and developed an understanding. Furthermore, Michaël spoke of the Indians being very spiritual, with a strong affinity with Mother Nature.

He spoke of the modern day problems and how man needed to wake up to the realities of the damage he was doing to nature through materialism.

Joseph and Michaël spoke of trading with skins and that they felt privileged that they had the trust of the Indians. Peter asked about the French soldiers but was told that they came later.

They spoke of the beauty of their world at that time and that they stored meat deep under the snow.

Their people's lives were spent chopping down trees and sending them down river for the purpose of manufacturing and the work was very hard but rewarding.

Fine Feather Introduces Himself

Christmas 1991 was almost upon us and the circle took a break until January 1992.

Various other personalities had spoken from time to time, through Melvin, me and Mollie but on the evening of 21 January 1992 Mollie felt a 'great power' with her. She felt weighed down and had to close her eyes. Her hands and arms felt very heavy and she was made to lean to one side.

She asked if there was anyone with them and Melvin's contact said that it was Black Eagle.

When Mollie suggested it was White Eagle, someone who had previously communicated through her, she was told that he had been White Eagle but had done a bad deed and had been renamed Black Eagle as a punishment and sent across the river near the outpost on the perimeter of the tribe.

No one was allowed to speak his name.

Asked what his misdeed had been, he replied that he had stolen some furs. He was well known at the outpost and had committed many misdeeds which had not been found out although Joseph knew but covered up many of them.

Michaël had no knowledge of this. The year was about 1750.

Mollie then asked if there was someone else with them and Black Eagle replied that there was a powerful figure with her.

Mollie said that she felt 'very strange' and Black Eagle replied that he felt it could be a 'new beginning'. He said it was the 'wisdom and power' that was bending her over.

Mollie felt that she could not watch the circle while she was so overshadowed and asked for more protection while she was in this state.

Black Feather said that he had asked again and again for a name of the new visitor but had been forbidden to use the name.

Perhaps Michaël might know?

Michaël then spoke quite clearly, 'Fine Feather', who was a strong man and very powerful.

He was Alan's guide and was giving power.

Black Feather said that he had known of Fine Feather but was never allowed to use his name, adding that Fine Feather was one of the 'Holy Ones'.

It then became clear that it had been, and was still, Fine Feather's power that had enabled Michaël to speak.

As the evening drew to a close and after much conversation about the events of the evening, I revealed that I had been told of my guide, Fine Feather, about five years previously through another trance medium, but had thought no more of it.

I had been to see a Spiritual healer who also happened to be a trance medium.

Along with the healing, the healer also gave some very good evidence of life after death over many months.

Sometimes we would receive direct communication from the healer's guide whose name I remember was White Horse. He once told me that I would be doing healing and mediumship one day, to which I replied that it was most unlikely as I had no interest in either.

One evening, White Horse was speaking and suddenly stopped to tell us that there was someone with the healer who wished to speak to me personally.

His manner changed totally and then a booming voice shouted to me, 'You sleep, you sleep!' while thumping my shoulder with the palm of his hand!

Somewhat shaken by the experience, I replied that I wasn't asleep but was wide awake listening to what was being said!

However, he repeated 'You sleep, you sleep!', once again, explaining in his own way that he meant I was doing nothing to enable him to help me to be a medium and a healer, and that we both had much work to do. I remember telling him in no uncertain terms that I wasn't interested, but it is quite apparent now that Fine Feather had other ideas.

At the circle held on 4 February 1992 Mollie again felt a very heavy presence after asking for guidance on how the circle was progressing.

The word 'tested' came to her mind. She then felt completely paralysed, could not move and could not open her eyes.

All she could hear was what follows.

You are being tested, have patience and bear with us, all will be revealed in time. We are extremely pleased with you and wish you to continue in the same way. The results will be beyond your wildest dreams. I feel this power is something very high, so high that it cannot reveal to us a personality, if you understand what I mean.

We are being guided by the very highest, a power so high and so advanced that it no longer has a personality, just this tremendous power.

It is a beautiful power, peaceful, loving, bright, and I feel we are in extremely good hands.

11

The Spirit wishes us great love and joy. It says whatever any of us endeavours to do with all our heart and soul for the Spirit world it will be of the best. It says that we are four very evolved souls and have been chosen for this purpose.

I feel great power around us this evening and we have been greatly honoured. The love of this power is overwhelming and I feel arms going out from me and surrounding all of us with tremendous love and great understanding.

I feel near to tears and yet there is great joy. They are tears of love and happiness. If we could see all the lights in this room, I don't think we would believe it for they are great lights of Spirit.

Once again we are left with the words, 'Love, Patience, Trust', and the great blessings of the Great Spirit.

A Major Breakthrough

For the next four weeks the circle continued sitting but with little of great interest. Then, on 17 March 1992 a new visitor made himself known, through Melvin. When asked who he was, he replied that his name was Andreus and he had lived in Britain in Caesars's time. He said he had been a centurion in Britain when on earth during the time of Boudicca.

He was asked who the Roman Governor in Britain was at that time and he gave the name 'Paulinus Seutonius', and he lived in Britain around AD60.

You can imagine our excitement when we later checked the Encyclopaedia and discovered that the Roman Governor's name was confirmed and that he was credited with having defeated Boudicca in AD60 or 61. This gave us conclusive proof, as if it were needed, that we were receiving communications from the Spirit world as none of the circle members would have known the name of the Roman Governor at that or any other time in history.

The circle continued for several months with various levels of activity and visits from other people in Spirit.

I felt that Fine Feather had been with me on a few occasions, perhaps as an observer, but had been unable or unwilling to speak, despite being encouraged by the circle members.

Later, in September 1992, the name of Golden Hawk was introduced to the circle and we were told that Fine Feather was helping him to communicate.

Fine Feather, being unable to speak through me at that time, probably due to my inability to allow myself to go fully into trance, decided to communicate through Mollie.

Mollie felt 'he was a huge man', about 6'-6" tall and very broad, with a very fine head dress.

He said he had wished to be spoken to but no one had, so he eventually decided to speak, himself.

This he found quite amusing. He then said that he hoped I would not feel 'slighted' by this but he wished to welcome our new friend to the circle and let us know he was there.

He then spoke encouragingly to us before taken his leave.

The following week all energy was concentrated on me, as Melvin wasn't present.

Our new 'friend' tried to communicate but only managed to give his name, 'Golden Hawk'.

Golden Hawk continued to try to speak through me into October but only managed the words, 'Alan will not go'.

It was clearly becoming a battle to get me 'out of the way' (i.e. allow myself to be taken further into a trance state), but I suppose lack of trust and maybe nervousness, prevented it happening.

(It takes a great leap of faith for an aspiring medium to allow a Spirit entity to take over ones senses to the extent that the medium has much less influence over proceedings).

Fine Feather appeared but only tended to nod and acknowledge questions, but it was obvious to me, due to the feelings he had (and that I felt), that Golden Hawk was someone special and even Fine Feather was 'very much the servant'.

On 3rd November Golden Hawk managed to get me 'out of the way' and although still a struggle, managed to speak. He is clearly a very old man and his voice reflected that, but he gave his name, said what a pleasure it was to 'be here tonight', saying that 'it had taken so long'.

Golden Hawk had the voice of a very old man and tended to shake quite a lot – that is to say, he made me shake, and said he had much to say to us.

(Being made to shake is one method used by Spirit to build up the energy required for them to work through a medium).

The following conversation then took place –

Mollie: Have you managed to get rid of Alan?

Golden Hawk: No (shaking).

Mollie: Why is it we all feel so protective of you Golden Hawk?

Golden Hawk: I bring a lot of love and you return that to me.

Mollie: I feel a great love for you.

Golden Hawk: It is a great help for me to know that you wish to love me. You have talked about my age amongst yourselves?

Mollie: Yes we certainly have.

Golden Hawk: I am very, very old. I lived hundreds of moons.

Mollie: Hundreds of years ago?

Golden Hawk: No

14

Mollie: You lived over a hundred? That was a long time in your day.

Golden Hawk: A hundred of moons is not as you call it. Shorter than your years, it is ...I don't know...

Mollie: You don't know how to put it?

Golden Hawk: Hundreds of moons, it was a very long time ago.

Mollie: Do you remember how long?

Golden Hawk: I have no way of knowing how long ago, I have a lot of ...

Mollie: Take your time. It must be very tiring doing this. Have you ever been back to Earth in this way before?

Golden Hawk then appeared to weaken and withdraw.

Soon Fine Feather started to communicate and the following conversation began –

Fine Feather: I am Fine Feather, Golden Hawk has gone away for a while. He will return to talk some more. He will have much to say. I am here to keep the link open. I am pleased to have been allowed to talk to you.

Mollie: We are pleased to have you.

Fine Feather: It is a great pleasure.

Mollie: Alan has found it difficult to allow people to speak through him.

Fine Feather: It is getting easier, I have worked on Alan for many years.

Mollie: Since he was a young boy?

Fine Feather: For five years I have helped him with his healing; he is doing very well in his work. He has been well rewarded already. He is working to help in our mission to open eyes all over the world and overcome much of the world's problems, it will take some time but we will succeed where others have failed.

Mollie: We have many problems in our world today. We hope we can help.

Then the energy started to change again –

Mollie: Welcome back Golden Hawk. Have you had a rest?

Golden Hawk: (Nods)

Mollie: We've had a nice conversation with Fine Feather.

Golden Hawk: The light is a lovely shade of gold, it is special. It comes from the highest source of life. It is working in our circle and it will continue to shine in the moons to come.

It is a wonderful source of help to you all and I cannot praise you enough for what you are doing in your circle. I have to leave you soon. I am pleased to have made a good impression on you tonight. I will be back again as soon as I am able.

Mollie: Thank you for being with us, it has been wonderful.

Golden Hawk: It has been my pleasure. I bid you goodnight and God bless you all until we meet again. I am going now.

Mollie: Goodnight, dear friend.

Fine Feather then returned, thanked us and bid us all goodnight.

We all felt delighted at the progress that had been made at this circle tonight and couldn't wait to continue next week.

The circle held on 24th November 1993 was very sad.

Both Golden Hawk and Fine Feather spoke about Melvin being unwell and his need to see a doctor. They both said that he would not return to the circle. We also received a bit of a lecture about how, in our world, we did not look after our bodies and when we became unwell through our own lifestyles, we expect the healers in Spirit to help us.

The following few weeks tended to concentrate on Fine Feather teaching the circle how to be more open to the influence of Spirit as he and Golden Hawk were having trouble communicating with us due to lack of energy.

The conversation sometimes became a little 'heated' because Fine Feather wanted us to work together more often to help build up the energy, but our material lives along with work and family commitments did not allow it.

From this date onwards, we found that much of the circle time was taken up by things of a similar nature – world affairs, the desire for peace etc.

That is not to underplay the importance of what was being said by a number of guides, and certainly not to understate what is often neglected – the 'miracle' of communication with people in the Spirit world. But for the purposes of this record of events, it is best not to be repetitive.

Trance Circle - 30 March 1993

The circle began with our very old guide, Golden Hawk speaking with a very strained voice through me, complaining that we did not dedicate enough time to our spiritual progress. Mollie remonstrated that we have very busy lives and our time was limited. The conversation continued in this way for about 10 minutes.

There was a long pause and then Fine Feather introduced himself.

I am pleased to be here. I'm waiting for Golden Hawk to refresh himself. He was overdoing the work tonight.

I am pleased to hear that you have been helped in your lives because the circle will benefit from that help, your lives will be more harmonious and therefore the circle will progress.

Peter will be more active within the circle in the weeks to come.

We have allowed him to get away from us, and he has benefited from our healing guides but the time has come for him to work and work he will.

He will make you all aware of your guides, one by one and they will work with you to make the circle progress in ways that you will not yet understand. It is not easy to explain the ways you will progress, but much progress will be made in the months to come and enhance your powers of persuasion in ways of encouraging belief in the Spirit world.

We must break the mould of your more orthodox religions before we can come to the fore and open the way for our philosophy of life.

But there will be an awakening of the minds of other people and your governments will be forced to listen and change their uncaring ways, where too few get plenty and the masses get little. There will be gradual progress and I feel that it will happen in your lifetimes on the earth plane.

The problems of your world are caused by the governments of your world. They have much self-interest that must be exposed and eradicated, and the people will be guided by the Spirit world but will not necessarily be aware of that guidance.

The world is going to wake up to the realities of the Brotherhood of Man and not a moment too soon. It is a very large task we have set ourselves but it will be achieved and achieved for the better, but not without pain. Many people will suffer in the transformation of your world in that they will

17

sacrifice their lives for the purpose of bettering the lives of those that remain in your world and their sacrifice will not be in vain.

The war is between materialism and brotherhood, and the brotherhood will succeed as materialism is defeated, but it need not be a war in the sense that you speak.

Those who believe in the cause will expose themselves to the vested interests of the governments, and they will be taken and removed from the spheres of influence that they inhabit. Thus they will influence others to rebel against the governments and force them to open their eyes to the realities of life, that they cannot continue the corruption that they encourage at the expense of the masses of people whose eyes will have been opened by the Spirit world.

There will never be perfection but we will achieve much in the interests of the people.

The governments are corrupt and will therefore fall when their corruption is exposed, and the people will decide that enough is enough.

Fine Feather then stopped suddenly. After a short silence Golden Hawk returned.

I am Golden Hawk, and I have decided to speak to you. He (Fine Feather) *has over stayed his welcome and I was waiting to return, to continue. You have learned much tonight. I'm not too sure that I would have allowed you to learn so much.*

Fine Feather is rather headstrong and he needs to learn that he must be more discreet when he speaks to you. But now that you know, I will not take the other way and I trust that you will not spread that knowledge too wide, because if it becomes known to the wrong people it can inhibit our progress and make our task more difficult to achieve but we will achieve that which you have been told.

I'm not prepared to elaborate beyond that.

You must continue to help our progress. Other people in other circles are receiving similar instructions and we will one day combine in a way that you cannot understand, but we will combine to influence those who hold power in your world. And the changes will be all the better. There will be no war as such, there will be peaceful protests at given times and given places that cannot be ignored by your governments and from those protests there will be influence of more people to our cause. The power will grow and grow and will spread far and wide.

That will be hard at times but those hard times will generate feelings that will have never been known before. Nobody wants war and therefore war will not happen, people have no desire to kill, they have desires to help one another for the common good and they will be helped by our influence.

18

That is as much as I intend to say.

Mollie asked that, having lost some circle members, if we should invite more people in our circle.

Golden Hawk: That will resolve itself in time.

I cannot say whether you should or shouldn't ask individuals to join but I am aware that you have a person in mind and I believe it is a woman and she is wanting to progress and will do so in time with or without your help. I would be happy for her to join your circle and I would not wish to decide when.

Mollie again asked who she should invite.

Golden Hawk: That is for you, you must ask your helpers. The power that we need will be depleted if the numbers reduce and that will hinder our progress.

Mollie pointed out that finding people with the right commitment was difficult.

Golden Hawk: That was to be addressed and you will find the people within your present circle of friends.

The circle then continued with questions about when to sit and how often, but Golden Hawk just reiterated that it didn't matter what day we sat, they would always be there.

He then said that he was beginning to tire and had to leave, saying 'God bless you'.

Trance Circle - 6 April 1993

The circle began with Golden Hawk speaking about the church celebrating the beginnings of Modern Spiritualism (Hydesville Day), the previous week.

Golden Hawk: ...the energy generated by the people was very apparent in our world, and we used that energy for the benefit of all the people. All those who attended were happy to be of service to that church and they must be harnessed for future events. There is much work to be done and the energy that was apparent that night can be used to benefit the Spirit world but it must become a regular event for us to use the power for the common good.

There will be some changes at the top of your church.

There will be beneficial changes and we will help those who initiate those changes. There are too many negative thoughts that must be removed and it shall be done but not in a detrimental way to those people, but in a natural way.

There is a feeling that those in charge are tired of their duties and they would wish to be replaced if they were to be honest. They recognise that there are new members in your church who have the benefit of the church in mind and they will be given their chance, in time.

Because as those changes occur, the movement will benefit also, and the Spirit world will become involved in the running of your church, and those who are chosen to take over will be mediums and healers, all of whom have proven their worthiness in that they serve the Spirit world with love and with the benefit of the people at heart.

This will come about in the near future and when it does there will be some bitterness from the present hierarchy even though they know that it is for the better. But they will continue to offer their help when they feel it is necessary, and the benefits will show them that it is best to continue being helpful to the church.

(Mollie expressed doubt and surprise at the suggestion.)

Then there will be many reasons to celebrate the new dawn that is coming. There will be a chain reaction around the world, that will be inspired by us and then our influence will grow and grow until there can be no doubt as to the power of Spirit.

This will bring about many changes in our lives on your side and ours because there will be a blending of our lives and interpretation of our words, that will work for the common good of the people.

I can assure you that the benefits will be worth fighting for but in the literary sense. The progress you have made in your circle has been repeated all over the world and there are many circles achieving wonderful things and they will merge as I explained before, and then the idiosyncrasies of the world will be defeated.

Then a new age will begin. I am tiring and I must withdraw.

After a long pause, Fine Feather then introduced himself:

Good evening, I am Fine Feather I have heard what Golden Hawk has spoken and I am surprised that he told you so much having told me off for saying the same last week.

I related to you the same views that he has shared with you and he chastised me for doing so.

But that is of no real consequence. The important thing is that the knowledge you have gained will come to pass in time, and I will be here to guard and guide you all as you make your progress in the way that you have been told.

It will be for all of you to use your knowledge for the benefit of the church and of the religion, as you call it. But discretion is the byword for progress must be gradual and peaceful or there may be a reaction that will not benefit anyone, and will make our task more difficult but not impossible.

Later Fine Feather spoke of the present church committee.

The present committee do not inspire any confidence in their congregation. They try to suppress the religion rather than promote it. There are no inspirers amongst them. They sit and talk and talk but I wish more people would shout their mouths off as you do. I have offended Mollie (who by now was on the committee), I think.

I apologise. I refer to the older members of the committee. They are happy to boost their own egos and not to boost their church and that's why there is no progress.

Mollie remarked that she is working on the platform a lot (as a medium and speaker), and hopes to promote the religion that way, and can't do that and work in the church to the extent that I'd like to at the same time. We all have problems of our own.

Fine Feather: There are many reasons why you are working for the church and they are recognised by us in the Spirit world, but your pathway is being prepared and there will be some changes in your lives, responsibilities that will be of benefit to you and your helpers.

Mollie: We can only do so much.

Fine Feather: Yes I do appreciate your problems but you will be guided. I realise that you have limited time and your priorities will be sorted out by us and ultimately by you.

We give you choices and you make your decisions.

Mollie then pointed out that working at other churches, for Spirit allowed less time to work at our own church.

Fine Feather: Mediums are very important in that they inspire others by their selfless work and if they continue to serve selflessly, others will come to come forward to reduce the burdens.

Mollie: At the moment, we have a job to make up a committee!

Fine Feather: That was caused by a lack of inspiration from the top. There is much to be done by your younger members. They will follow if they are guided, and they in turn will inspire other people. They are developing their own mediumistic skills and that will prove an inspiration for others.

Mollie then spoke of modern life being so busy.

Fine Feather: They do not spend their time wisely and they will be guided to develop their interest in the Spirit world if they have the inspiration of others. Much of their spare time is wasted on trivial things and they are seeking for something better and their reactions to their inspirers will prove that they have found what they were seeking, something better.

I feel tired, I will retire.

God bless you all.

Trance Circle - 20 April 1993

Once again Golden Hawk started the communication, remarking that *'there were few present tonight'*. The energy was not strong as a consequence.

He decided to allow others to speak because the conditions were too difficult for him to work.

Fine Feather then began speaking about the circle being important and others will combine in the future to ensure progress.

I was having to give up the circle because of work commitments away from home (I was about to begin a six month contract in Birmingham due to a shortage of jobs in London and the south east), and Mollie was concerned about the progress of the circle without me, seeing that it was through me that Fine Feather and Golden Hawk spoke.

Fine Feather found it difficult to satisfy Mollie's fears about the future of the circle but continued…

Fine Feather: We do our best in poor conditions to help you progress and to develop your work and to tune into our vibrations.

Mollie felt that sometimes we felt we weren't 'getting there' and were stuck at a certain point.

Fine Feather: You are not stuck at any point, you are making progress gradually and will consolidate you progression.

Conversation continued in this way for a while.

Fine Feather told us we make our own decisions with help from the Spirit world, and as time goes on the Spirit world are able to guide us without us making specific requests. As each individual person progresses, then the next person will receive more guidance than he had previously received and in time you will all meet at the same level.

Fine Feather: I have concentrated on Alan and he has progressed a long way. I am aware that he wishes to do more within the church and Alan is restrained by his working conditions and that will be resolved too.

There are many problems with your world with regard to the availability of work for the people and your society has conditioned itself to regard that as a problem.

Mollie: Yes, but we do need money to live on, unfortunately.

Fine Feather: I might not necessarily agree with that statement.

Mollie pointed out our need to buy food and pay for a roof over our heads.

Fine Feather: We managed to live in your world without money and my life was all managed right.

Mollie continued to speak about our material needs although she said that some people are self-sufficient.

Fine Feather: There are conditions that have been man-made and have made money a necessity and those conditions can be 'bended'. You can ...the power is fading...I will have a rest and you can continue. I will return.

Fine Feather later returned and remarked that he was impressed with the conversation that had gone on while he rested, remarking that he was particularly impressed with the dedication of each individual and that they all progressed at different rates.

Continuing from his previous talk, he said that in his time on earth there was less need, less selfishness but they had problems of a different kind.

Fine Feather: We developed a spiritual pathway of life. Our need to involve ourselves in the life of man was pre-empted by the pathway that man chose to follow in the latter part of this century.

A pathway of selfishness, greed and competition between man has not been beneficial to vast numbers of people, and we had to be involved to perhaps, correct the errors of the those people who were not totally convinced that that was the way man wanted to go.

They maybe went along with the principles but had more of a conscience about the effects of their actions on others, and they were trying to endeavour with our mission to return to the spiritual way of life.

There are many people questioning the virtues of the political systems that have developed around the world and they chose to look at ways to improve the lot of the masses rather than their own lifestyles and they are now effective in promoting that attitude.

Young people had not had time to be indoctrinated and that is why we have made progress with our message. They will form a vital part of our mission to promote a world with a better message than is being promoted by your leaders.

They are frightened that those who 'have not', will demand what they want from those who 'have' and they will not need to be forced to share their wealth, they will do so willingly, and as the uptake of that change in attitude increases, things will change for the good of man and the Spirit world will have accomplished its mission. At that point we will retire and leave things to those enlightened people to promote the benefits of that way of life.

We can do only so much. Man must realise that he has responsibilities to others and not just to himself and we can allow him to exercise his free will without so much influence from us and that will be a lesson for man to have learned from the mistakes of others.

We have endeavoured to promote a way of life to your people with some success but now we can gradually depart from being totally functional in the progress of your world.

I am tired now. I shall depart.

God bless you.

Unusual Spirits in a Public House

In early 1993, Pat Robertson (the church circle leader), who knew about our progress outside the church circle, received a phone call asking if we could help to sort out a problem at the Hare & Hounds Public House on the A23 at Waddon, just outside Croydon.

She told us very little of what she had been told by the family running the Hare & Hounds, except that they believed there was 'Spirit activity' and that it was very unsettling.

Pat, Mollie, Ted (a church member and healer) and I decided to see if we could help.

So we arranged a suitable evening to attend and, on arrival, were shown to a room in the attic, which was just along the corridor from some bedrooms. We asked to be left alone for an hour or two, while we attempted to find the cause of the problem.

As we sat in a small circle in the middle of the room, a prayer for protection and guidance was said followed by a period of silence as we waited for something to happen.

After about ten minutes it became obvious to the others that I was becoming entranced by a Spirit entity and Pat asked who it was and if he wished to communicate with us?

Using my voice box, a very gruff and angry man started to speak with an aggressive tone.

He was asked to calm down a little as we were there to help him, if only he would tell us what his problem was.

It gradually transpired that this was the spirit of a man who used to live in this room a couple of hundred years ago.

(The pub was on the main London to Brighton Road and had been a coaching inn used as a stopping point for weary travellers en route).

He obviously hadn't accepted that he had passed over to the Spirit world and was therefore still living in 'his room'. He complained that people were coming in to his room, 'moving things and interfering with his belongings'.

When asked who these people were, he replied 'them boys'.

He was then asked,' how many boys?' and replied 'two'.

(This was particularly good evidence that we had genuine communication as Pat had not told us that the landlord and his wife had two sons, who were frightened of going into that room or indeed, the corridor, because of seeing this horrible looking man and that items had been thrown in their room).

The conversation continued along the lines of clarifying what the man's problem was, followed by informing him that we were now in the 20th. century, and not the 18th century during which, he lived, and telling him that he no longer lived in that room but had passed away.

After much persuasion, he was asked to look for a light that would guide him to a much nicer place, where he would find his loved ones waiting for him. He eventually became aware of this light and as he was drawn closer to it, he became very emotional and thanked us for helping him.

Pat then found herself being 'taken over' and began speaking in a very deep, ladies voice with an Irish accent, (Pat is Scottish). She too had a very aggressive tone and, like the man, had lived in the room for a couple of years a long time ago and wanted it back for herself.

A similar conversation as before ensued, and the lady progressed towards the light.

A much more emotional situation then began, when Mollie was taken over by a young lady, who said she'd been a maid at the inn many years ago and her accommodation was that room.

She had been 'taken advantage of' by the, then owner of the inn and had become pregnant by him.

Not wishing to bring shame upon himself, she was confined to her room from the time the 'bump' started to show, until the baby was born, again in that room.

After the birth, the maid died without having seen 'her baby' and had stayed close to the room after her passing hoping that she would be allowed to see him.

A very emotional and tearful conversation then took place during which it became obvious that we had assistance from the Spirit world to enable her to 'move on'.

We continued to pacify her and told her that if she looked for the light, her baby would be there waiting for her. With intervention from the Spirit world, she became aware of her baby, and cried, 'my baby, my baby' as she gradually moved towards it and further on into her rightful place in the Spirit world, with her long lost baby.

We were later told that the couple's young daughter had seen a lady and said that 'a lady had asked for her feeding bottle for her baby'.

To say this was an emotional experience is an understatement, but such a worthwhile experience.

It soon became obvious that as the coaching inn must have had hundreds, if not thousands of people passing through it over the many years of its existence, we could be here all night, dealing with similar cases.

So we said a prayer for any other lost souls that may have been present, and bade them farewell. We then went downstairs to explain to the landlord and his wife, what had occurred and they confirmed a number of things to us that had not been discussed before.

We never heard from them again, until our curiosity got the better of us and we phoned them to ask if all was well.

They told us that the atmosphere was now very calm and 'normal' and no further problems had occurred.

The Mystery of the Teddy Bears

A few months after the rescue work at the pub we received a phone call from a married couple living on a new housing estate in Belmont, Surrey asking if we could help solve a problem which had bothered them since they had moved into their house some months earlier.

The couple had no children but the wife had a collection of teddy bears which she placed on their bed each morning after re-making it prior to both of them going to work.

On their return they often found that the teddy bears had been moved around the bed, and sometimes had been thrown around the room.

In addition to this, the living room was always cold, no matter how much heating they had on.

So, once again, we set off to see if we could help, as much out of curiosity as concern for the couple.

We asked the couple to leave us alone in the living room while we sat in a circle and, after opening in prayer, we sat quietly hoping that we would receive communication from the Spirit world.

After about ten minutes, Mollie and I became aware of a young female energy which was slightly in awe of us, as we were of her.

Speaking through Mollie the girl revealed that she had lived in a property that had existed a century or more ago. It had been a type of orphanage run by a kindly gentleman who owned a stately home set in large grounds. He took in children who had been orphaned or abandoned and gave them a home and an education.

The young girl spoke of having been very happy there until her passing at the age of about seven or eight, after a short illness.

She'd had a teddy bear and had 'left it behind' at the house. So, in her eyes she was simply returning to the property in which she'd lived to retrieve her teddy before she moved on into the next stage of her life.

In doing so she was rummaging through the teddy bears on the bed and leaving them in a mess for the couple to find.

Her presence in the house was also creating the coldness the couple felt in the living room because that is where she spent most of her time.

29

After a short conversation with her, we were able to gain her trust and encourage her to look around her for someone who might be holding her teddy bear for her. She gradually became aware of a shadowy figure in the surrounding light, who attracted the girl with a strong sensation of love and was seen to be holding a teddy just like the one she had left behind.

Gradually the girl was able to move towards that light, and she recognised the person holding the teddy as the gentleman who'd looked after her all those years ago.

This was a most emotional event to witness and a few tears were shed as she turned and thanked us as she waved goodbye and joined her loved ones in the Spirit world.

After we'd finished our work and closed ourselves down, thanking those people in Spirit for their help, the couple returned to the room.

Their first remark when they entered the room was 'how warm it felt' and that 'it had never been this warm before'.

We related the story to them of the young girl and her circumstances during her life and they confirmed that the site on which the new housing estate had been built had indeed, been the grounds of an orphanage and a stately home during the 19th century.

We left the house very pleased with the work we'd done and agreed that it was quite amazing that we were able to have solved the problem through our own mediumship and with the assistance of those who help us from the Spirit world.

We had been told that we would be helping the Spirit world in ways that we would never have thought possible when we began our circle, and this was now beginning to happen. It seems there are many people who can't accept that they have passed over from the physical world and remain close to familiar earthly surroundings waiting to be helped by people working together on both sides of the veil.

Holy Water Causes Anger

As we became more able, with the help of our Spirit guides, to clear houses of 'Spirit activity' it seems we were being used more and more to assist in the work of our Spirit friends to enable 'lost souls' to accept their circumstances and complete their journey into the next stage of their 'eternal progress'.

Now and again we would receive a phone call from people who had discovered our church and asked us to help explain a 'presence' in their house. When we visited them to find out more, it soon became obvious that the caller either had a vivid imagination or had been under the influence of 'spirits' of the bottled variety.

Because of this we decided to be a little more cautious and asked a few more searching questions before giving up our valuable time to help possible time wasters.

After all, we didn't know what we might be letting ourselves in for by going into strangers houses without vetting them.

However, after a call in 1992 from a man living in Elmers End, near Beckenham, Kent we decided to attend because, by the fear and worry in his voice, there was an obvious need of help.

The owner of the house, a policeman, told us that he felt that there was a presence in his house which he and his family found unnerving.

As well as 'cold spots' in the house which made a room feel cold even when the heating was on, there were unexplained noises such as knocking and scraping sounds coming from upstairs.

Things gradually got worse when objects started to move for no obvious reason and without anybody being close enough to cause the movement.

After tolerating these things for some time, the owner contacted the vicar at his local church for advice in the hope that he would be able to do something to stop these strange happenings.

The vicar visited the house and set to work to do what he could to communicate with the spirit entity and command that he must leave the house and the owners in peace.

The vicar then proceeded to scatter 'holy water' around the ground floor of the house shouting, 'depart evil Spirit!'

The homeowner told us that as he was doing this, he was soaking the floor, the furniture and anything else in the rooms, but not only this but after several minutes of the vicar chanting 'depart evil Spirits', the policeman was picked up by an invisible force and thrown the length of the hall from the living room, crashing into the front door!

He was obviously in great shock and swore to us it was true.

This was even more remarkable when you consider that the policeman was over six feet tall and very well built so it would not be humanly possible for him to be picked up in this way let alone thrown about fifteen feet.

The vicar then decided to make a hasty retreat from the house, but returned at a later date with the local bishop in the hope that someone of a higher order might be able to help.

However, the two working together just seemed to make the cause of the problem even more irritated and they left the house in great haste after a very short time.

The policeman then decided to contact Croydon Spiritualist Church to see if we could be of any assistance.

Incidentally I was later asked by a reverend acquaintance of mine, 'do you know how they make holy water?' I replied that I didn't and he told me, 'they pour the water into a saucepan and boil the hell out of it!'

When a member of an orthodox religion feels able to mock their own methods I feel vindicated in having a more 'common sense' approach to these problems

However, I digress…and so it was that we found ourselves being told about the strange goings on in this house and realising that the owner and the family were reaching the limits of their tolerance.

Our team consisted of me, Mollie, Peter and Ted. Ted was a healer at our church and provided a lot of energy for our work as well as being very relaxed about holding conversations with our Spirit friends when they spoke through me when in trance.

After our conversations with the homeowner we asked him to leave us alone in the living room, which appeared to be the main centre of Spirit activity and the coldest room in the house.

He provided us with four chairs and some water after which he left us. We began with a short prayer, asking our guides to draw close to us with their love and protection, asking specifically that no one of ill intent should get close to us. Then we sat quietly.

Before long my breathing became much deeper and more drawn out and gradually I was taken over by Fine Feather.

As usual, Fine Feather formally introduced himself to us and the others returned the greeting. He explained that he was aware that there was a presence in the house but the individual Spirit was not evil, she was merely a 'lost soul' who had become aware after many years in the Spirit world that she was going nowhere and could not go back to her physical life. She felt that she needed to go forward to 'somewhere' but had no idea where and how to progress.

By making herself known in the only way she was able to, causing a nuisance in the house, she achieved her objective of making the homeowner seek help.

Fine Feather then 'stepped back' as it were, allowing the individual to come forward and speak through me and explain who she was and what she wanted.

She was unable to give a name as she had been in the Spirit world for so long, but she remembered the incident with the vicar and confirmed that she had reacted with anger to the vicar's command to 'depart evil Spirit'. The young girl had objected to being labelled 'evil' and summoned all the energy she could to make the vicar leave.

Our conversation with her revealed that on the site of the estate there had been a children's home of some kind many years before and the girl had lived there. She was made to say her prayers daily and attend her local church against her will.

She gave the impression that she had been badly treated as a result of her not wanting to attend prayers and had therefore taken a dislike to religion generally. So it was no wonder that she had reacted so aggressively to the vicar's commands and his assertion that she was evil.

She went on to tell us that she felt 'trapped' and knew that she had to progress away from this in-between state she now found herself in. She had had brief glimpses of light shown to her but was a little fearful of responding to them. With our help she was encouraged to look once again for the light and to realise that we were there to protect her along with our guides who were with her in the Spirit world.

She hesitantly looked around her until, at first, she saw a faint glow of light in the distance.

Still a little hesitant, we asked her to look for someone in the light, perhaps her mother or father, and gradually she became aware of a shadowy figure approaching her. As it got closer, she remarked that she could feel a greater sense of warmth within the light and that she felt a wonderful feeling of love surrounding her as she recognised the approaching figure as her mother.

As she became more comfortable with the experience she became very emotional and thanked us for helping her to make the full transition into the world of Spirit.

The emotion generated by these experiences is such that the other members of the circle also experience much love from the energy created and it is impossible to put into words the feelings that we share. I can only say that if you try to describe a scene of natural beauty, your words cannot do it justice.

It is the same with rescue work.

After the individual had left us for her new life in the Spirit world, Fine Feather returned to thank us for our work and promised things would now calm down for the family in the house.

The policeman attended church services a couple of times after we'd been to his house and told us that all was now ok and things had calmed down.

We then heard no more from him, despite asking for an update on the situation after perhaps a couple more months, but he didn't bother to contact us, which suggests to me that once the problem is dealt with, the work of the Spirit world (which to my mind is a minor miracle), tends to be taken for granted.

Or perhaps he wanted to leave well alone, thinking that by contacting us things might start all over again, after all we do believe that 'thoughts are living things'.

Trance Circle - 18 May 1993

Golden Hawk wanted to communicate again but was struggling to speak and make himself understood.

As usual it was Fine Feather we waited for, and after hearing briefly from others, he eventually started to speak through me.

Fine Feather: I am Fine Feather, I am glad to have been allowed to speak to you tonight. I am pleased to be here.

There are many things that are not understood in your world.

We continue to grow and grow and will continue if we have your trust in the Spirit world, and progress is only made when we stop and obey our instincts within our hearts.

We all progress at different rates and our progress is hindered by doubt and questions. I have no more to add to that, but I thought it needed to be said.

Mollie: Are you saying that in our world and also in the Spirit world, do people doubt?

Fine Feather: At every level there is a measure of doubt in the minds of that individual and until that doubt is removed progress cannot be achieved. It is as that on our level as on yours and our progress is hindered by doubt.

There are many worries and there are many emotions and combining them is an act of reducing the worry.

But when a worry is alleviated, then we have plans and then we progress and that is all l can say.

Mollie: Well, we only learn from our worries.

Fine Feather: ...and from our mistakes, and I might add to that, that we all mistakenly worry.

Mollie: It is a vicious circle isn't it?

Fine Feather: However that is not the purpose of our circle. I'm not quite sure why I am here now?

Mollie: We are very pleased to have you here. You do not have to have a purpose to be here.

Fine Feather: I'm prepared to wait and see what transpires...

35

A short period of general conversation and intermittent silence then began and then Fine Feather returned, just to close the circle.

By this time it was becoming quite obvious that what we were experiencing was something quite special – some might say miraculous. Having conversations with people living in the Spirit world is quite amazing, and we felt that we should share these experiences with others of like mind.

However, despite wishing to put on a public demonstration, our material lives tended to take over, with personal problems, long hours of work and other distractions, we were unable to do so.

The circle sat from time to time, and contact was maintained with our guides, particularly Fine Feather, but we were unable to dedicate ourselves in the same way we had previously done.

In 2000 my circumstances changed and we were once again able to devote more time to trance sitting.

In early 2001 we felt that which we were receiving was again, too interesting to be confined to a small circle, so we decided to present a public demonstration of trance, but in front of an invited audience only.

So on Saturday 2nd June 2001 a demonstration was presented in the presence of members of other churches in the area.

This was firstly to test me to see if I could remain entranced for long enough to gain experience and lose my inhibitions, and also to make it a worthwhile experience for those present.

We were not to be disappointed.

Trance Demonstration - 2 June 2001

Croydon Spiritualist Church

An invited audience of about 30-35 people attended the event, including church members, serving mediums and visitors from other churches.

Mollie and Pat Deverell sat either side of me to provide energy and to protect me.

I gave a brief talk before settling down to prepare for the demonstration, giving the audience an opportunity to hear my normal voice and observe my usual mannerisms.

This was followed by a short opening prayer given by the church president, Mrs. Mollie McManus. (Note the change in the church hierarchy which had been predicted in 1993).

After about ten minutes, my guide began to speak, as follows.

Fine Feather: Good Evening my name is Fine Feather.

We have waited for a long, long time, for this opportunity to demonstrate the power and the capabilities, of those of us who reside in what you call the 'world of Spirit'.

We have patiently waited for Alan to develop and progress, and perhaps, dedicate himself, more than he was once able to do, and to work and speak for us.

We have invited you to witness the wisdom that we wish to demonstrate, for it is plain for you to see...for us to observe, that the world in which you are living, is suffering so very much.

You are not directly responsible for that condition. It is not the responsibility of any one individual or group of people.

The condition of your world has been permitted to evolve without any influence from our world. We have observed and permitted you to use the freewill that you all possess and learn for yourselves how things can be allowed to develop for better ...and for worse.

There are many very, very good people in your world who are screaming within, within themselves to do, or will others to do, that which must be done to improve the quality of life for so many impoverished people. Why do you scream within?

37

Why do you scream within, when there are so many waiting for the leadership, from people of like mind? A leadership that demands something will be done, to alleviate hunger, warfare, pollution...need I go on?

The will is there for you to tap into. For you to stand up and perhaps, be one of those who speak for the majority and please believe me when I say you will be speaking for the majority.

The leadership of your countries, your continents are barren, spiritually barren.

They believe in power only for the sake of power, and while they exercise the authority they possess, they continue to work only for the minority. They must be contained.

You have in your world, witnessed revolutions, forced upon the majority of people as the only way to react to the leadership, the leadership that serves them so badly.

Those methods of revolution cannot succeed, for they generate more hatred and selfishness, so many of the things that need to be destroyed.

We are promoting a peaceful, progressive revolution. You cannot begin to understand our methods. But I can assure you that there will be a rapid progress, from this day on.

You may be interested to know that as I speak to you, others from my world are speaking in other parts of your world.

You don't believe in coincidences? That is no coincidence.

There is a concerted effort from our world to influence many groups such as this, all around your globe, and from this early, tentative step forward, we will slowly but surely generate the energy and the circumstances to allow your circles, your groups and your meetings, to unite, again in a way that you cannot understand.

But you will communicate across the continents. This will be the first step in showing how communication and influence can spread so, so far and wide.

Please believe my words, take them with you and share them with your friends.

Please believe them, for unless you do, nobody else will.

Your acceptance of my words is such an important beginning, for you will adopt a more positive stance and a more positive attitude, due to the understanding of the world of Spirit. We seek no reward and you are here because we know that you seek no reward.

There was a period of silence, and then Fine Feather continued...

Fine Feather: I was made to withdraw, please be patient. You will receive more from me, but I must withdraw.

Petrah will speak with you; Petrah is much more evolved than I.

My name is Fine Feather and I am never far away, my own guides use me, as you say, more and more, now that I have a working instrument.

My knowledge has wisdom. This is not infinite, shall we say.

There are others who are able to follow my light, my channel, seeking to convey their words.

So we have developed together you, Alan and myself.

I am very proud to have done so; a very, very productive journey.

I've only begun, you will participate far more than you have already. You will all work and gain in your own ways. Hopefully encouraged by this event, will progress with Alan and myself and with your own guides in the Spirit world. They are with you as I speak.

Fine Feather then withdrew and a second person in Spirit began to speak in a different, more gentle voice and manner from Fine Feather's. (This personality was new to us).

Petrah: Good Evening my name is 'Petrah'

I bring greetings to you from the many people around me who work with you, with you all.

There are many highly evolved personalities here, and among yourselves, each person has reached a level of development, understanding perhaps, and more importantly a desire, to work with and for Spirit.

I am not happy with that word 'Spirit'; I prefer to use the word 'soul'. The soul of a man is so important. Soul is that which is within your heart, your mind and your own being.

I have already told you of my preference, Spirit is a word used only to satisfy the vast majority of people within your world, who can perhaps better understand an existence other than your material world. But soul is a much more enlightening word; a much more sensitive word.

'SOUL'.

There are no hard sounds in soul and that, if I may, is how I shall address you from today.

Peace envelops everyone within this hall. A peace penetrates the hearts of you people who are so receptive to our world. So responsive to the needs of your world, and you build bridges between the two, blend with the energy that we provide, and share that energy with others with your healing, with your touching.

Touching both physically and emotionally.

Touching the hearts and minds of others yet to be enlightened to the possibilities that lie within their own being.

Touching, feeling and caring. Very sensitive but very strong words.

They may sound like words of weakness, but it requires strength to touch the emotions and lift the hearts and minds of people around you who are weaker. Strength to understand the needs of others and it takes strength to care enough to want to improve their conditions. Physical strength is nothing without the strength of the soul and you have that in abundance.

I trust you to use it and use it well. Take not rewards in your material existence. Seek not rewards other than the enrichment of your own soul, your own being and your own emotion and strength, as your only reward.

Perhaps I may be permitted to suggest that this, tonight, is a reward. You are privileged to witness communication from higher souls. Those who follow your progress and encourage you to put your knowledge to good use, and inspire you to use words which you may wonder from where they came. When you speak to others have you never asked, 'where did that word come from?'

Need I answer you?

Petrah then said that the energy was weakening but offered to answer questions before he withdrew.

When asked when he had lived on earth and where, he replied that he had worked in a monastery, but was not a monk. There was no materialism and fewer people in the world, who learnt together.

He remembered living in a warm, arid climate and wearing a long, white garment to keep him cool.

He was then asked if, when we pass to Spirit, we judge our own lives and come to our own conclusions about the life we have led.

Petrah: Do you not already judge your own life?

Experience is life. Some traits go with you when you pass, others will be discarded. You decide what level of evolution you will go to, and blend with the souls of like mind and experiences, and then judge yourself.

The final question Petrah was asked was, 'Is there such a thing as fate and does free will still have a part to play?'

Petrah: Fate encompasses your own thoughts and desires. You can, and do cause things to happen by your own actions.

Are things pre-ordained? Is that what you mean?

We must all experience many things in our lives. We adapt our lives to suit our own conditions. Peace, hardship, happiness.

How you respond to adversity develops your personality. Fate is not a suggestion that things are pre-ordained. But some things, such as, birth and death were pre-ordained.

Petrah then said that he had to return to his own 'level'.

Fine Feather then returned and said that he relished speaking to us.

He said he would return to speak to us, to work with me and to demonstrate the power, to show that they are sincere and not a figment of our imaginations.

He said that we were all willing participants and that more trance and physical phenomena would be witnessed, and that there was much work to be done together.

He then invited questions.

When asked, 'Are there seven spheres in the Spirit world?' he replied, *There are unlimited spheres. Infinity means nothing and everything. You will never cease to exist. If there were only seven spheres, where would you then go?*

He was then asked, 'The progression of physical phenomena was forecast 70 years ago between the two world wars. Now we are in a period of relative peace, is this allowing phenomena to come forward?'

Fine Feather: The existing skirmishes in the world will not be allowed to spread. They are being contained not only by the Spirit world, but by the nations of this world. Physical phenomena will play a part in the war on want in our world.

Fine Feather remarked that we did not need to work in darkness, but would be able to work in light so that all people could see the phenomena.

The next question was, 'Who chooses our guides?'

Fine Feather: We see a light and respond to it by our own level of development and experience.

If the person is willing to progress, the guide will not depart but will encourage and share his own experiences through a mental process.

We choose you, but in a way, you choose us by your light.

We consciously choose to work with you.

Fine Feather then thanked the audience for their questions and said, *'Goodnight.'*

41

I had been in trance for approximately an hour and a half, and everybody found it a very enlightening experience.

Because of the success of this demonstration it was decided that further demonstrations would be arranged, but in future, to anyone who wished to attend.

Trance Demonstration - 7 September 2002
Croydon Spiritualist Church

Once again, Mollie and Pat Deverell sat either side of me to provide energy and to give me protection.

I gave a brief talk before settling down to prepare for the demonstration, giving the audience an opportunity to hear my normal voice and observe my usual manner.

This was followed by a short opening prayer given by the church president, Mrs. Mollie McManus.

After about five minutes, my guide began to speak, as follows.

Fine Feather: Good evening, I thank you for introducing me, I usually introduce myself, good evening my name is Fine Feather.

It is good that you are here tonight, you will, I am sure, have your own opinions of what you observe. You will take home many interpretations of the philosophy that you will hear.

That is good, you cannot all agree upon those things that stretch the limits of your minds, you all have the free will to take from these words that which you desire.

The people on my side of life have observed many of the services, call it what you will, within this church, with growing enthusiasm and greater interest than elsewhere. They support each of you in your endeavours to satisfy yourselves that there is continuous existence, and by continuous I mean infinite.

There are subtle differences between those two words.

Infinite has no beginning and therefore no end. Continuous implies certain limitations, I shall not define them; time does not permit.

You will never, ever cease to exist.

Physically you shall, but spiritually you will progress into infinity.

Your light will grow ever brighter as you continue to understand the realities of life, the realities of the energies that exist between this world, my world and other worlds, some of which I have no understanding. For like you, my development is not complete.

Petrah, another of Alan's guides and a great influence on me will be speaking to you very soon.

Petrah is far more highly evolved than I.

My purpose has been to persuade Alan to progress and work for the good of your religion. He has been inconsistent in his desires to concede to my will, but, we have ways of persuading and cajoling and how you say, encouraging people to submit to our will.

The light that you all reveal to us, the light of your soul, your Spirit, enlightens us to the type of person you are. That light is of use to us when we choose you to work for us in whatever way we feel is best for you.

We cannot persuade you if you are determined not to travel the road. That is your choice. But we can encourage you to perhaps, meander away from the pathway you choose, with gentle persuasion.

Your free will is open to manipulation, but you must remember that you chose the life you choose to lead before you became a shell around your Spirit; and that is all that you are.

Your Spirit survives many changes, many environments, many habitats, all of which offer opportunities to learn and evolve and work towards the infinite that you call, 'God'.

I am aware that there are many on my side of life here tonight, many, many people, more than you on your side. They wish to work, they wish to draw from your spiritual energy; the energy within this hall, to show you what they are capable of showing.

I began by suggesting that you will decide what it is you wish to take from this event.

It will be for you to decide if you have witnessed a visual experience, a visual event tonight.

Some will imagine, some will see and some will wonder.

Question, that is good. It is good to question.

Satisfy yourself in your own time that which you can begin to accept and slowly you will progress beyond the questioning into a state of mind that allows you to accept.

That will then mean you have progressed to a point where we can use you and you can be used for peaceful purposes, and that, that word alone, is a word that passes the lips of so many people in your world...peace.

Work with us, work with the many other groups that work around the world and peace will be achieved.

You find that hard to believe?

From my experience, from the work that we do, I have to persuade myself that it is as you know, that I do observe some progress in many parts of your world who request peaceful solutions to ongoing problems.

We are making progress, we are moving forward with our ultimate aim to achieve what you call recognition in your world, and through that recognition we can certainly persuade others in your world, whose minds are locked against our existence.

We can provide the proof that they need to move away from their misdirected aims.

That day may be far off but you can play your part by experiencing for yourselves what is happening before you. I thank you. I will return.

I must withdraw. God bless you all.

Petrah then began to speak.

Petrah: Good evening my name is Petrah.

Petrah is a name I was given on my entry into Spirit, my name was not Petrah when I was with you.

I have no knowledge of my name, for it was never used. My work within the monastery was less exciting and very varied, but we were made to observe rules, and one rule was to remain silent for many, many long periods.

My time here was short compared to your physical lives, but I worked within the monastery, helping the monks who dedicated themselves to observing, in their way, the world of Spirit.

I was never able to join them. My work was to feed them, clean for them, work in the fields to produce food. I never was able to achieve the enlightenment that they achieved.

My enlightenment came, when I joined others in this world; one I must confess I did not know existed.

I do now.

My work with the monks enabled me to progress spiritually by providing for them, so you see there are many ways that you can work in the aid of your spiritual progress.

You may wish only to observe, you may, but you will pass on what you have seen to others.

That is working for your spiritual progress. Do not feel you cannot achieve other achievements.

There are those within this church tonight who will confirm that nobody who is here working for the church, nobody initially believed that they would be in such positions, and yet they are here, working to bring you the proof, as you say, of life after death.

I say life continues; death is not a word in my vocabulary. Death is nothing but the closing of the doors of your physical bodies as they become of no use to you in your spiritual progress, and you will leave this world all the better for having had the experiences you have had.

Good and bad in your words. All good in mine.

Good experiences envelope so many of your material lives, and even what you call bereavement, where you hunger, pine, for the physical return of your loved ones, but, we see that as a good experience.

Some of you will understand that, I'm sure.

Some of you here benefit from having had the experiences of losing your loved ones.

Some of you will not understand what I am saying, but, each time you lose a loved one, you perhaps get a glimpse of a life beyond this physical life.

You get a glimpse of the light that burns within your mind that generates itself through your body and nourishes your inner being, nourishes your spiritual side and makes you a better, more understanding person, so that others can benefit from your experiences and you can show compassion built upon your experiences.

Can you understand my words?

Can you understand that nothing is wasted, nothing is of 'no use' to you?

All experiences are good in that they nourish your personality, your soul, and nourishment is what makes your spiritual soul evolve?

Peace is so evident within the walls of this church, I feel almost surrounded, swamped perhaps by the love that envelopes us all.

Can you not feel a gentleness; a feeling of being loved, around you?

Can you feel that energy?'

If you can you are well on your way to understanding how energy works. Collectively we generate the love that will eventually merge with others of like mind, and that link of love cannot be broken. That is the purpose behind your spiritual work.

Peace will never be achieved while you are led by vested interests, your churches, your governments, your monarchies.

These are not working for world peace.

The existence of your churches, of your religions, is like a fuse, a touch paper igniting the conflict between the people whose only differences are within their minds.

Their minds are controlled, you must believe that, and you are receiving a similar dogma which you choose to ignore, because you have seen the real light.

You have seen what is beyond your physical minds.

You cannot be dictated to anymore, for you questioned and received your answers.

The archaic religious structures that are being constructed within your world are barren of ideas and ideals.

They exist merely to support the hierarchy that grows in physical strength, and loses the credibility when they try to talk of mythology, and many of you will know what I speak of.

They have built myths around perfectly ordinary people, and you are made to worship in their name.

Those people who were only highly developed souls, sent here to help you, to help you know that material existence is not all, and then the stories were changed and political and religious hierarchies grew and dominated the thinking of illiterate people.

There are few illiterates in this world now, most people can, and do question and think for themselves. Can you now see that those hierarchies in time lose their credibility and many of your religious structures will collapse because they cannot stand on one word – truth?

Truth is all you need to focus people's minds.

That which you witness tonight, therefore, believe me when I say you are walking a common pathway and that pathway will lead, as my friend Fine Feather has told you, towards a world of peace.

But not, I might add, in the lifetimes, the physical lifetimes of some of you.

You will depart from this life in the knowledge that you have aided the efforts of people on both sides of life and your light will shine ever brighter in this world.

Peace envelopes all of you in this church.

That is collective desire and that will continue to spread. You will see.

I need a break; the energy is good, very good. I will ask you to observe, it may be of benefit to reduce the light above me, you should still be able to observe those of us on the platform. You may feel you have seen enough of us.

Anyway, expand the depth of your vision, allow yourselves to experience what we can do with your energy and I trust that some of you, perhaps all, will observe something.

So I shall withdraw. Please reduce the lighting and I shall return and perhaps question you on your observations.

God bless you all.

The lights were subdued and the congregation were asked to observe any changes that might occur during the next 5-10 minutes.

Petrah: May I suggest that some of you saw my face change, and you might have recognised the face upon mine…I hear no response.

Members of the congregation reported seeing Alan's face change.

Petrah: Perhaps you were observing my surroundings rather that my own being, therefore, were you able to observe anything unusual?

Sheila: He disappeared!

Petrah: I did de-materialise, I wondered how Alan felt, for he found himself in darkness, there were shadows visible to you?

Geoff: I saw shadows.

Petrah: Those were others around me who wish to witness your lives. You must understand that you are a curiosity to them. They are curious and they have always believed in you, but now perhaps you believe in them.

Those of you who saw shadows, did you observe things behind my back?

Were there auras around some of the shadows?

Audience: Yes!

Petrah: That is good, a faint, very faint glow was emanating from those who desire to see their loved ones. There are one or two bereaved people who would love a glimpse of one who shared their lives. Continue to observe and you may observe a face within this vicinity. Please speak if you do notice a loved one and feel free to speak to them, and you will perhaps experience a visual reaction, a physical visual response, please observe and I shall withdraw once again.

At this point a man named Jack started to speak, in a cockney accent.

Jack: Who's that, who's that?

Mollie: They are very nice people come here to see you.

Jack: Are they with you?

Mollie: Yes they're with me, all my friends, they're nice aren't they?

Jack: What they doing here then?

48

Mollie: They are watching you, come to see you.

Jack: Me?

Mollie: What are you doing here?

Jack: I'm just here, I'm always here.

Mollie: That's interesting

Jack: Ain't seen that lot before.

Mollie: They're here regularly enough.

Jack: Why do they want to see me?

Mollie: Who are you then?

Jack: I'm Jack.

Mollie: Jack? Jack who?

Jack: Gawd blimey does it matter?

Mollie: Yes when you say you are always here, where's here?

Jack: I'm here, just here ain't I? Where are you, you're here ain't you?

Mollie: We're sitting in a church.

Jack: A church get out - a church?

Mollie: I'll tell you further than that, it's a Spiritualist church.

Jack: Right where did you learn about that - a church?

Mollie: Tell us about yourself Jack.

Jack: I don't want to, now what people am I sitting with here?

Mollie: Oh we're ever so friendly.

Jack: I worked on the docks.

Mollie: When was that?

Jack: Blimey a long time ago, boats everywhere'.

Mollie: What did you do on the docks?

Jack: Up and down loading, unloading, bloody hard work, long hours too.

Mollie: What happened to you Jack?

Jack:..Got beaten up, had a bit of money, had a drink then I left, I was here. Where are you from?

Mollie: We're in Croydon.

Jack: Little town, pokey little place really, ain't it?

Mollie: I suppose it was at one time, big place now.

Jack: Oh, is it?

Mollie: Where did you live Jack?

Jack: Where did I live? Do you know Wapping Wall? Nice there, nice little house. Kids, pub down the road.

Mollie: You liked your drink?

Jack: Yeah, thirsty work.

Mollie: What was the pub called?

Jack: Pub? Had a lady in it, had a lady on the sign. The Blue Lady. The Blue Lady.

Mollie: I don't think it's there now.

Jack: Where have you been?

Mollie: I don't go in pubs much, especially in Wapping.

Jack: Ain't there now.

Mollie: Did you go back and have a look?

Jack: Yeah, knocked it all down, nice it was.

Mollie: What year were you alive----Queen Victoria?

Jack: Queen Victoria who's she. Victoria? We didn't have a Queen then.

Mollie: What did you have then, a King?

Jack: Yeah, it's got be one or the other ain't it?!

Mollie: Which King was it?

Jack: You're having me on aren't you? You're having a laugh you are.

Mollie: Well we like having a laugh, I bet you had a few laughs when you were here?

Jack: Yeah you gotta, working hard all the time. George someone, George III.

(George III reigned from 1760 to 1820. He was mentally unfit to reign for the last decade of his life and his son, George IV acted as Prince Regent until his father died).

Mollie: Good heavens you're going back a long time.

Jack: Didn't care really. I think it was George.

Mollie: George III, goodness me.

Jack: Why what year is it now?

Mollie: Do you want a shock? It's 2002.

Jack: Oh yeah, get on 2002?

Mollie: It is, no wonder you said Croydon was a funny little town, it was in those days, and it was a village.

Jack: Farms, it's alright here ain't it?

Mollie: Yes it's alright here, lot worse in the world.

Jack: Got to be happy.

Mollie: What do you do in the spirit world?

Jack: Well I just get on, walk about, meet me mates.

Mollie: You still meet your mates?

Jack: Oh blimey yeah.

Mollie: You still go to the pub?

Jack: If I wanna yeah, I don't work so hard now, easy life.

Mollie: You've got your wife with you?

Jack: Yeah, she's still around you know?

Mollie: What's her name?

Jack: Can't lose her, she's alright. Mary's her name.

Mollie: Mary, old fashioned name?

Jack: Nice girl, she's nice. Old fashioned what's old fashioned?

Mollie: Got a few kids in Spirit world?

Jack: Yeah, getting on now though.

Mollie: Got a few grandchildren and great grandchildren?

Jack: Yeah, nice actually, get out and about.

Mollie: You enjoy it, you'd recommend it?

Jack: Yeah, get out of here, it's heavy here, I feel heavy.

Mollie: You feel heavy?

Jack: Yeah, I'm not a big bloke.

Mollie: Since you lost this body it's a bit lighter?

Jack: Lost me body, what you talking about?

Mollie: Well this body the one we're sitting here with?

Jack: I got a body, I see it. I see yours, (pause) funny lot...!

Mollie: Yes we are a funny lot really. You are not the only one who thinks we are a funny lot.

Jack: Well it's up to you if you want to mix with them. I can't stay around here any longer.

Mollie: Have you got work to do?

Jack: Well I've got to get on, can't hang around here.

Mollie: Where are you going?

Jack: I've never been to church in me life!

Mollie: Where are you going to now?

Jack: I'm going home.

Mollie: You're going home, thanks for coming. We've really enjoyed having you. Hope you come again sometime.

Jack: Didn't know I was coming tonight!

Mollie: Goodbye Jack, God bless you.

After a short period of silence, I began to become aware of Petrah returning.

Petrah: I am back, greetings, much energy tonight. You have observed I am different; I speak wiser, you may have noticed there are many people who have not changed'.

Your friend, Jack?

He has no desire to move from his level, he's happy.

One day he will observe the brighter light and aspire to investigate, but he's happy.

Very peaceful here, it is good, I cannot stay. I must return.

I think Fine Feather will answer questions. He will return and so shall I.

God bless you all.

After a short period of silence, I began to become aware of Fine Feather returning.

Fine Feather: Greetings once again, I see many surprised faces.

We like to surprise you.

I have been given the privilege of asking you if you wish to ask questions.

I shall try to enlighten you within my current understanding. You may ask.

Question: Fine Feather what do you look like or what do you feel like?

Fine Feather: I feel energised by you tonight, I feel as solid as my instrument, my friend Alan. Within his being, his shell, I feel heavier, lighter, how can I explain. I am lighter; the light of my being is lighter in your world than in mine.

52

Your energy of your world suppresses my light when I enter this body. My friend Alan does have a picture; he has refrained from asking if that picture is of my likeness. I will tell you, it is, and I ask you to ask him to reveal it to those who have not observed it.

I can only emphasise that I had a fuller face than that within the picture, but the features are a good likeness. I hope I have answered your question.

Question: How long have you been a guide?

Fine Feather: I have been a guide; I have always walked with Alan. I have observed his behaviour, his physical growth and by his light I was drawn in.

Therefore, I have always worked to influence Alan's progress, his desire for fair play.

He sometimes wavered from the path but he was permitted to do so. Free will is important.

Before I attached myself to Alan's spiritual body and physical body I worked with others collectively, developing my own soul, helping many people to make the transition from your world to ours, and that included mass destruction of life in your wars.

We were there to greet them, to help them, and know that they were safe.

That is part of my growth and experience.

Are you aware that my voice has changed (the voice sounded like Petrah had returned).

Petrah: Fine Feather withdrew so that I could explain the workings of life in Spirit.

He chose to call me to return, I found myself talking once again. He has withdrawn; there is a blending of our souls. That is why he experienced a gradual change, so gradual you didn't notice.

We live in a strange world; he has many thoughts, but very powerful energy. I can take a question.

Question: Are my mummy and daddy happy in the Spirit world?

Petrah: Everybody is happy in the Spirit world, but happiness you know, is a state of mind. Happiness is within, it's not without.

You can think yourself happy, you can think yourself sad.

A state of mind, so your question perhaps was immaterial because I think your happiness was defined as materially.

It is within your mind you will find happiness.

Still your mind, meditate, relax you will find happiness.

I feel although the energy is strong, your time is an obstruction, therefore, I shall withdraw.

I think Fine Feather will return, God bless you all.

Fine Feather (somewhat agitated): I was made to withdraw, I allowed him to come back. His wisdom is greater than mine. I allow him.

I must return, I thank you for being here this evening. I do hope that you have learned much and seen much.

You will continue to help yourselves by helping others.

God bless you all.

Trance Circle - 30 January 2003

Good evening I am Fine Feather. I am very happy to be with you.

So began another interesting evening.

Mollie: It's been some time.

Fine Feather: I regret that, I wish to have more opportunities to speak. I shall endeavour to achieve my desires.

There are many things I wish to discuss with you. You are few tonight, and you will not be surprised that I chose that you would be as you are.

I am disappointed that you have one fewer than I wished.

Mollie: Pat Deverell (past Vice President) is missing.

Fine Feather: You are right, she will be attuning, I feel. She is very dedicated, more than she ever was.

Working hard, working well, helping others, and indeed working with us. Her motives are very unselfish, very caring and very helpful.

She too receives guidance from me and from her own guides.

We are a very big and strong team of workers, on your side and on mine. That is why we achieve so much and the achievement will not be compromised by mischievous elements.

We are very strong; we have a very powerful shield of resistance, powerful beyond your comprehension. It is as if arrows try to penetrate the thick wall that is impregnable.

Not all your mischief makers are without sincerity, some work with their own guides, some work with sincerity, choosing to impose their desires upon the minority within your church. But their desires do not compare with the opinions, desires and needs of those who benefit most from your achievements, your efforts, and your desires.

I choose the word desire, for ambitions are not to the fore.

Ambitions imply egotistical desires.

Ego does not enter into your thoughts. Ego does however drive desires of a few, and they will learn from their mistakes. They will continue to influence those who are easily led, easily influenced. They will succeed but the impregnable wall that we have built will prevent any damage, because the strength of your spiritual growth overrides any material advantage that these people, these souls, will gain.

(At about this time there were a couple of individuals in the church who were responsible for creating problems by gossiping about other people with the intention of creating disharmony, and this had yet to be addressed).

Their spiritual growth is uneventful, therefore.

I would suggest that you all pay attention to your own desires, your own requirements, and your own achievements. Do not be distracted by, I will not say misguided, but by misunderstanding people. People who would return to the failures of the past; failings of the past, where progress was hindered by weak souls.

People chose a quieter life rather than set out to make their own mark upon the proud name you call Spirit. They chose to sit, they chose to sleep, and they chose to rest, they chose the easy option of allowing your church to stagnate.

That will return if those few people influence a minority and are permitted to continue to influence the way they do. They will not be permitted to do so. They are trapped within their own material wall; material instincts override their spiritual progress.

They criticise, they complain, they argue, they achieve nothing. They will achieve nothing in the days to come.

Their energies will be weakened, their energies absorbed by their own material instincts. Therefore, their spiritual progress will stagnate. Therefore I can only emphasise the importance of progressing along the road we have set for you.

We are walking together towards enlightenment that you have dreamed of.

An enlightenment that will overwhelm the weaknesses of the few.

An enlightenment that will cause people to shed the tears of joy and that they will see for themselves the power of the spiritual way.

The power behind the light of Spirit.

The power behind the world of (how you say)...you have peace movements. They are praying, seeking intercessions from a higher order. They are pleading with their own religious faiths for an answer to the continual desire by some to cause conflict; by some to cause inequalities, by some to retain their material levels of existence.

Your peace movements are spread far and wide; they are a minority in such a way that you as Spiritualists are a minority.

I ask you to remember the minority exists only in voices of those prepared to speak, only in the numbers of those who choose to speak for the majority.

Behind that hierarchy there is an extremely large minority waiting for a sign of leadership.

A sign that they are not alone, that their thoughts are shared by many, many more than appears to be the case.

I will say that those who choose a life of conflict; choose to threaten others, choose to allow hunger and poverty and homelessness in your world, which has resources for everybody, those people are the minority.

But they are a powerful minority. Very powerful, but there will be a time when the power of good, power of unseen forces, unheard of forces will penetrate into the gloom and fog of your world.

That is why I suggest that many will weep with joy. They will fall to their knees, not in worship with false idolatry, not with false homage, but with weakness before a powerful energy exuding extreme amounts of love compassion and peace.

I cannot find the right words to describe to you that which will befall your earth.

It is something you cannot begin to understand, but there is to be a return to a more spiritual way of life.

Materialism has served a purpose, your physical wealth, your ways of living are far, far better than they once were, but now the time has come to destroy the inequalities that materialism has created, and make those in power, those who perpetuate the inequalities, end the wars that derive from those inequalities.

It is time to finally accept defeat. They are fighting against a tide of spiritual rebellion, spiritual reaction. That tide cannot be turned back.

I have explained to you many times before, you are one of many groups around your world, but you will one day connect and join together in a desire for peace. Then you will see the crumbling of the walls of power, you will see the power of Spirit, of God.

God's influence will be everywhere in the light that will shine on everybody.

Inequalities will slowly evaporate and peace will once again endure in your world.

Do I hear you say, 'Dream on?'

Mollie: Will it be in our lifetime?

Fine Feather: Your lifetime is eternal, you will witness these events in your eternal life, and I cannot promise in your material life, but whichever side of life you exist, you will continue to play your part. Do you not see around you, see a great reaction against war that is being planned?

(War in Iraq was being discussed at this time).

You will not have witnessed such a reaction in past times. The cause is not just; the cause is one of greed. Excuses are made to antagonise and intimidate others to support the war. They are very transparent excuses. Therefore, can you not see that we do have influence.

We can help you at this moment, and you will find something will happen that will prevent a conflict on the scale that is being planned.

There will be reactions from other parts of your world which will cause your leaders to rethink their strategies, for there will be serious consequences if you are allowed to proceed.

We can assure you that there will be a satisfactory conclusion to the conflict, but, that conclusion will not be satisfactory to everybody important.

There will be a counter threat from another source causing your leaders to think again.

I suggest that as you are recording my words that you retain this copy of my words and you will be able to confirm that I was correct.

I already sense a more relaxed atmosphere within this room. There were tensions within you all, I feel. I have relieved them to some extent.

Can I offer assistance in any other way? Please speak.

Mollie spoke about a problem in church and how to deal with it.

Peter (Mollie's husband): Rise above those problems and control your own emotions; discretion better part of valour.

Fine Feather: I agree with your words. We have asked you to trust in Spirit, we ask you to share your problems with us and you repeat those words to others.

We hear you say 'trust in Spirit.'

Your reaction to, shall we say, less evolved people, should be to ask them to look within themselves, to trust their own instincts, their own inspirations. Ask them to look within for the answers to things that trouble them, and then walk away.

Allow them to ponder, allow them to quietly, secretly change their minds.

Do not impose any of your thoughts, but suggest that they look within; they will see a glimmer of light, a glimmer of inspiration, a glimmer of hope. I find a word, 'rectitude', I do not understand.

I suggest they will see...I hesitate...the error of their ways. There are no errors, they are learning, they are seeking without wisdom. They will discover wisdom within themselves.

58

They must be inspired to seek it by looking within themselves, for if you attempt to impose upon them, thoughts they cannot appreciate, they will continue to react against them.

Reconciliation found by suggestion, rather than imposition, and that is an answer to the problems of your world, as well as your personal and private problems. A suggestion is preferable in this position.

Mollie: We get tired, too tired to cope with problems.

Fine Feather: May I suggest that everybody within this room must at times take that advice. My instrument, yourselves, you must all seek guidance in everything that you do, and I will suggest that my guide Alan is probably the worst... (much laughter).

We have much guidance available to him if only he would ask. He must ask. I cannot impose anymore, ask him to look within, there are many answers to many of his problems within himself. He cannot find them. They will present themselves if he asks.

Mollie: I react to problems and then quieten down.

Fine Feather: I began by speaking of others who choose to criticise and cause problems.

They are undisciplined. They will hit against a barrier of their own making because they choose not to look within. They are going full circle.

Discipline.

May I suggest when problems present themselves; I think you speak of your circle; your answer to those who speak out should be as I have said. Look within yourselves for your own answers and you will know they will be intimidated by that statement. They will be upset, maybe, but if they are made to look within and they are a minority, they will know what to do.

Mollie: Upsets in circle by individuals; upsets everybody.

Fine Feather: I suggest that you ask people to leave their problems at the door. May I suggest that you begin by repeating that, and those who have ignored that request be asked to depart until they are able to do this.

Mollie: It upsets 20 people.

Peter: People who attack you, ask them to look within. Thank you. You have done a great service for me this evening.

Fine Feather: Say it with humility and not superiority, then turn away. You have the wisdom now and the knowledge.

Progress...I will enlighten Alan one day. He has some news to come, he will receive some news.

He knows... I cannot lose him completely, he is still here with me but he cannot speak, I cannot allow that. He will receive some news, he is seeking an answer but he will receive some news.

I cannot elaborate beyond that. There is something of importance about to be revealed and then he will move forward. He is stagnating. You are all progressing well. You are all progressing as you must and only as you can.

Peter: I have great trust in Spirit when working on platform.

Fine Feather: That is good, there are many in your church, many in your circle who aspire to that level of trust, but they must be allowed to progress. In time they will see their inner light and respond accordingly.

Peter: I want to convey my feeling to you for what trust means to me.

Fine Feather: Therein lies the source of the world's problems, mistrust, evil emotion, it is time for me to return. I shall return sooner than you expect.

Mollie: Your appearance on platform was well received.

(Fine Feather had chosen to override Alan's planned address when taking a church service).

Fine Feather: Thank you, I cannot always be there to speak. I will be when I choose. There are some occasions that justify a higher mind. Excuse my description, a higher mind than Alan's and sometimes a higher mind than my own, and it will be on such an occasion when you have an audience who need answers, that you, Alan and other people cannot give, on those occasions I will be speaking, and there will be an occasion very soon.

I shall look forward to that occasion as I always do. I am frustrated by my lack of progress; my progress is hindered by Alan. I cannot force him to work, but I will remind him of his obligations to me as well as to others.

His conscience is working in my favour.

I must go.

God bless you all, I thank you for the opportunity to speak tonight.

Violent Passing Causes Spirit Return

With the occasional but regular demonstrations of trance and the experience gained, it was becoming much easier for me to allow myself to be 'taken over' by Fine Feather and as a result our rescue work, although less frequent, was becoming easier to deal with. That is until the spring of 2003 when a lady named Dee phoned with a problem.

She explained that she lived alone on the ground floor of a purpose built block of flats in South Norwood and had often felt a presence there whilst sitting watching television.

She hadn't thought too much about it until one night she felt there was someone in bed with her and she felt she had been touched. When she turned on the light, she found there was no one there physically, but she certainly felt the presence of someone in her bed.

Obviously this was becoming more and more distressing for her, so much so that she could no longer stay there but moved in with a friend.

Dee's ethnic origins were the Caribbean and, being a member of the Evangelical Church, Dee attended her church one day and told the Minister what had been going on in her flat, asking him if there was anything he could do to help.

He informed her that it was an 'evil Spirit' and that she needed to be 'cleansed'. He asked her to attend a service where he would do what he had to do to help her.

Dee duly attended expecting that prayers would be said for her benefit.

After the regular service had ended, the Minister asked the congregation to remain seated and quietly meditate as he had a special problem to deal with. The congregation did as they were asked and the church became a haven of peace and quiet as all present began their meditation.

Not realising that this was for her benefit, Dee became very relaxed as she drifted off into her own little world.

Suddenly without warning, the Minister, who had by now crept up behind Dee, started hitting her about the head while shouting at the top of his voice into Dee's ear, 'DEPART EVIL SPIRITS, DEPART AND LEAVE THIS WOMAN ALONE!!'

The object of this exercise, presumably, was to frighten the 'evil Spirit' away, never to return.

However, the unintended consequence was to frighten the life out of poor Dee, who jumped out of her chair, ran out of the door and never returned.

Needless to say, the problem in her flat, which she still occasionally visited to collect her mail, continued unabated.

In desperation Dee contacted Croydon Spiritualist Church and asked if we could help as her nerves were shattered and she really wanted to return to live in her flat, but until this 'presence' was removed, there was no way she could return.

Soon after, on a Saturday afternoon we paid Dee a visit.

Unfortunately Mollie was unable to attend and so the group consisted of me, my wife Pat, and our dear friend and vice president of the church, Pat Deverell, who has since passed to the higher life. This was my wife's first experience of rescue work and she was a little worried about what to expect.

Dee explained what had been going on and was clearly very upset and distressed. She asked us to do whatever we had to do to get rid of the problem so that she could get on with her life.

The worst of the activity centred on her bedroom and we asked that she leave us alone in that room while we set to work.

The room was quite small but had a double bed, with a wardrobe and chest of drawers, with little room for the three chairs we needed to sit, so I sat on the bed while the two Pat's sat on chairs.

Not an ideal situation but the only way we could work.

The curtains were drawn to put the room in darkness and we sat together in the usual way, saying a prayer for our guides to protect us from those of ill intent and asking that we may be of some help in solving Dee's problem.

As we sat, there seemed to be a long pause before we felt the presence of Spirit, but gradually the atmosphere in the room turned from peaceful to one that can only be described as nasty.

(I hesitate to use the word 'evil' as it tends to be overused by members of other religions, but the atmosphere certainly became very oppressive).

In my trance state I knew that the entity taking me over had an aggressive nature and the two Pat's sensed it too, saying afterwards that they feared for my safety.

Eventually my body became very tense as the man taking me over began to speak in a very aggressive way, clenching his fists as though he was about to lash out at anyone close enough to be hit.

He started to shout, 'Gerrout of here, gerrout of here' in a strong south London accent. 'Gerrout of my house. Gerrout of here.'

At this point the two Pat's were feeling quite threatened, but having complete trust in our Spirit friends, Pat Deverell began to speak calmly in an effort to gain the trust of this man who was clearly very angry and wasn't prepared to go anywhere.

It took a while but eventually Pat managed to calm him down.

By this time my body was shaking uncontrollably with the energy the man was taking from me and I was sweating profusely.

My wife, Pat told me afterwards that she feared for my safety but trusted Pat Deverell to deal with it.

Slowly Pat asked the man to try to relax, if only for my benefit, so that a conversation could begin with the intention of helping this poor man.

Pat asked him questions about his life when he lived on earth and it gradually transpired that he had lived in a room in a three storey property that had been demolished to make way for this block of flats in the 1960's.

South London had lots of such properties in Victorian times as 'well to do' people tended to live there.

Some of these properties were demolished as a result of wartime bombing in and around Croydon, due to the close proximity of the strategically important Croydon Airport, and in the 1960's Croydon had a large rebuilding program.

However, this man's last memories were of having lived in the property years before and in his eyes Dee was now trespassing and had no right to be living in what he felt was his home.

But his story developed further, becoming quite tragic, which caused us all to become very emotional.

He was asked how he passed from this world and he told us that he had been out one evening to his local pub and was followed home by two men. When he arrived home, they pushed him into his flat and started to beat him, demanding money.

He'd tried to resist but because there were two men and they were much younger and stronger than he was, he was so badly beaten that he collapsed in his room and died from his injuries over the next few days.

It was several weeks before his body was found. His assailants were never found and that was the reason why he couldn't leave this world as he hoped he could somehow cause them to be brought to justice.

It is perhaps, no wonder that this man still had an aggressive nature and was causing Dee so many problems.

The rest of this rescue became such an emotional experience that it took a lot out of me, as I was still in trance and under the control of this man.

Pat Deverell managed to calm the man down and made him understand that he needed to complete his journey to the next world. Although the man spoke only of being surrounded by darkness he began to relax and listen as he realised that we meant him no harm and wanted to help him.

Pat then spoke of the need to 'go towards the light'.

The man replied, 'What light?'

Both Pat's then spoke calmly to him and asked him to look around and he would see it.

If you can imagine that as I am under his control, it is my eyes he is using to see, 'I' am the one that is experiencing what he is seeing.

As he looked around he/I gradually became aware of a faint light, but also a peace that he had not experienced for so long.

With that peace came a wonderful feeling of love surrounding him, again, something he had not experienced for a very long time. Gradually, with Pat's prompting, he/I started to see a figure approaching him which he soon recognised as his mother, and the tears began to flow.

I began to sob uncontrollably as his emotions overcame me and he called out, 'Mother, mother', and she came forward to embrace him and lead him forward into the light and the love of the Spirit world.

He turned to thank us for helping him and bringing him peace at long last and then slowly disappeared into the light.

At this point I felt an overwhelming desire to go forward with him as the emotion and the love I experienced was something I had never felt before and it was only the gentle sound of Pat's voice calling me back, that made me remember where I was and that I had to return.

When I finally regained my awareness, not only was I soaked with sweat, but my tears had been real and had soaked my face and my upper body.

Once again we had successfully aided the transition to the Spirit world of someone who had been 'trapped' in a sort of in between place between the earth and the Spirit world, and I have to say that it is a very rewarding and humbling experience.

If ever I feared what happened at the point of physical death, these experiences have taken that fear away and I know that however and whenever I go, this 'tunnel of light' that so many people, having had near death experiences speak of, will provide me with a warmth and an overwhelming love to help me on my journey to the next phase of my existence.

Trance Demonstration - 8 March 2003

Croydon Spiritualist Church

'Good evening my name is Fine Feather; I am very honoured and appreciative to be able to speak with you this evening'.

Thus began another evening of 'words of wisdom' from Fine Feather.

Fine Feather: I wish to speak on the subject that you call Spiritualism.

You are all spiritual beings and you are here because your evolution, your progression is perhaps far more advanced than that of others. You have chosen to be enlightened by myself and by others who I hope will bless your church this day.

You may have believed that you chose to attend; you chose using your own free will. I must tell you that you were chosen.

You were guided to attend to learn and to add to your spiritual knowledge.

If you look back on recent events in your lives you will see, some of you will see, that there were obstacles potentially preventing you from attending. Those obstacles were removed, those obstacles, in my mind, were not important, and, therefore your guides, your friends, relations, your helpers were influenced; were influenced by my guides, my friends, myself, to enable you to overcome, perhaps, to side step your obstacles.

I cannot see but I know you are there and I ask my friend Mollie to acknowledge that some of you experienced that of which I speak.

Mollie asks the audience did they encounter any difficulty getting to the trance evening, a couple of people in the audience confirmed they did.

Fine Feather: Then you are providing proof of the power that we have upon your world and your lives.

That I hope will encourage you to believe and trust when we ask you to when we promote our beliefs our knowledge in your church in your lives.

You each will have experienced many things. You will have asked for help, asked for guidance and asked for healing. You will also be aware that your answers have been provided and you will be aware of a different answer to that which you expect.

I can only suggest that guidance you received was that which you required rather than desired.

Your desires are perhaps of a more personal materialistic nature. Your requirements enable you to learn to understand and to progress. Your requirements are nurtured, they enable you to help yourselves through experience, and, through your experience you are enabled to help others.

Is that not a desirable objective?

I can know of no other greater use of our spiritual energies than to help other people. In so doing you help yourselves, as you know, the more you give the more you shall receive.

Would it not be a desirable lesson for all peoples to learn from the Spirit, the world of Spirit, to enable them to prevent so many of the inequalities and what you call undesirable events in your world?

I have spoken in the past of the many things that we are able to do with your help. We cannot achieve anything in this world unless we have the unconditional assistance and knowledge that you can and will work with us, and you have all been chosen to work with us.

You may not choose to do so consciously but you are enabled by your acceptance of our survival and our energy, or power, if you like, to make changes where there must be changes.

I hesitate to progress onto the subject of your impending conflict I am aware that as I speak through my medium he wishes for me to speak of other things. He is aware that I continue to say things of a similar nature each time I speak.

He does not understand that I speak to many different people.

Many of you this evening will not have heard my thoughts on conflict and warfare and therefore I shall continue on that subject.

(At this time there were plans for America and the United Kingdom to attack Iraq and to depose Saddam Hussein).

You have in your world many, many conflicting interests, many powerful influences and many selfish people. Combined energies generated by those three states of being are causing many of your problems in your world, and may I suggest that you are able to influence the outcome of those events.

Now, I suggest some of you are disbelieving and unable to understand how, when you are mere individuals in a world of events, you must trust, you must learn to listen, listen with your mind, internally.

Within your mind we are able to communicate our thoughts, our desires, our methods, if you will listen.

Do you really believe that you are alone in your desires for peace, for equalities, for an end to hunger in a world of plenty, to an end to poverty, disease and slaughter?

Slaughter, a powerful word but it emphasised the extent of the damage that is done in the name of progress but in the pursuance of power.

Power is corrupting influence in the wrong hands. Power is a powerful influence for good when used by those who desire peace and equality within your world, and I cannot condone the leaders that you have in your world. I cannot condone their actions, for their actions are built upon very crumbling foundations.

As one person destroys another must rebuild.

Can it not be that you can choose people to lead your world to continue the rebuilding without the destruction?

To rebuild...the desire of people such as yourselves.

Build for the good of all and build with love, unselfishly. Caring not for oneself, caring not for ones prestige, caring not for ones ego.

I ask you, would you not feel safer, happier working together under leadership of peace loving, caring, constructive leaders?

I think I know the answer but we witness from our side of life the continuous destruction, hatred, killings in the name of God; in the name of Allah. Mere words, mere words.

God is a word. Many people use that word in their language, their speech without caring for the importance attached to the word God.

God the father, the father of all creation the father of all you perceive, of all you touch, all you feel, and all that you see.

God is your father and you are his children.

You have no label, no attachment to any other. You are guided by your thoughts. Your thoughts are energy; your energy is at one with God, for God is energy.

Some say God is love, love is energy. You give out energy when you speak of love, when you care for your friends, your loved ones.

When you hug, when you touch, you feel, you listen, you speak with love. You are using God's energy.

The opposite is hatred, selfishness and all things that oppose the power of love. It is of the same source, the energy is from God but I am able to tell you that that energy which is used for undesirable actions is a distortion of the energy provided from God.

It is distorted by the thoughts of men and women who work against their innermost desires. They fight against their own thoughts and eventually they progress to a selfish mind and uncaring actions.

Those distortions generate bad energy and it is becoming increasingly clear that those minds are increasing their power against humanity.

We are in ideological combat, therefore it is important that we of like mind combine our energies to force the negativity to retreat and I will emphasise again that war in your 'holy land', your war, can still be prevented if enough people are prepared to speak, to pray and force their desires upon the minds that speak of evil and hatred.

The power of prayer is a very powerful source of energy, it is a way that we are able to work to improve the lot of many in your world. Without your thoughts, your prayers, your sincere desires expressing themselves to us, we have nothing, nothing, and it is your light, the light of people desiring peace, desiring equality, desiring that those that have nothing shall share what you have.

Those people shed a light that we can see. That is why we appear to you, because we see your light. We are drawn to that energy. We absorb your energy; we amend your energy to progress our way to impress upon you that which we can do.

Energy can be re-used, channelled in different ways and re-used for the benefit of others.

You will not be able to understand how we are able to use your energy for you live in a world of matter, which you call solid matter. We live in a world of Spirit, as you say, of a lighter vibration, as you say...higher vibration.

Mere words, but we exist in a world that permeates your world, though you are unable to see, you are unable to hear. Most of you are unable to perceive, therefore how will you explain what you now see and hear?

Do you deny that I am a separate being from my medium?

Do you who know my medium, accept that this is not the man you know?

Do you accept that I am of a different order?

Please speak....(general agreement)

I thank you. Therefore will you accept that you too are able to achieve that which my medium has achieved?

You may not wish to do so, nor shall you if you so desire, but my medium chose the same many years ago. He told me, told another medium through whom I spoke, that he was not interested.

He was too busy, too involved in his material life.

I think I won!

It has been a long, slow journey but I was determined that he would work with me to improve.

I must choose my words to express my thoughts upon those who would listen, those who are willing to learn and understand the workings of the world of Spirit.

I have guided and helped in many ways, my own medium, but he has helped with my progression also.

For, you understand that as you give of yourselves you will gain for yourselves. That continues throughout your lives on this earth and within the world of Spirit.

Progression never ceases but I will confirm that you or I, having chosen my medium, having chosen to work with him, for him, and him for me, we shall continue together to eternity.

The bond of love, of partnership, the mutual desires will never be broken. We are as one in our thoughts and desires and trust is the greatest bond between us.

Without trust we could not co-exist and I have won my mediums trust but it was not easy.

My medium will not believe without proof. He questions, he studies, he works to disprove and is often surprised, though I don't know why, when he discovers what he sees and hears is true.

That is good; I cannot understand anybody who believes without investigating, without questioning, without a desire to understand the subject.

They are researching. It is important that you question.

Disbelieve until you have investigated and satisfied yourselves that what you have seen, heard or felt is true.

That way trust is built between people.

That way you may progress yourselves and that way, can you not see that if what I say is understood, all over your world, that trust will grow between men of all nations, all religions, all creeds?

And trust alone will help you to prevent warfare. The cause of your wars, your disharmony between nations, is lack of trust.

You cannot trust your leaders. Your leaders cannot trust the leaders of other nations and they in turn do not trust the motives of others who lead their countries.

Distrust is a negative energy, a powerful energy but it lies at the heart of many of your problems; of your personal problems and your world problems. Trust can only be constructed over time.

Trust your fellow man, people you know, and more importantly those you do not.

May I ask you to trust that we are sincere in our desires to help you, for we are here only to help?

We wish to build upon your personal desire to improve your world. Together we can achieve that aim over many, many years.

For it was many years in the making of your current problems. It will be many years of trust, mutual desire for peace; many years to correct the mistakes of your past.

We are at the beginning of a breakthrough. The breakthrough will reveal the innermost secrets of your minds, the innermost thoughts of your hearts, your desires, by using your energy you can manipulate others ...manipulate, the word I was searching for.

Manipulation is a steady progressive move forward when used for the good of all. That is why I ask you to continue with your prayers, your thoughts of love and harmony and enable us to help you and your fellow men.

Please hear my words. Accept what I say, for I am sincere. I am desirous of a peaceful existence within your world.

I choose to suggest that you share my desires.

I feel I have spoken for too long I feel that you may wish to hear others speak, to witness the power that others possess.

Therefore I shall withdraw. I thank you for listening. I shall return.

God bless you all.

There is no record of any further speaking on this recording.

Trance Demonstration - 7 January 2006
Croydon Spiritualist Church

Fine Feather: Good evening, my name is Fine Feather.

I am very proud and privileged to speak with you this evening.

My desire to speak is only to inspire you, and, to perhaps, encourage you to accept that there exists a life around a sphere, to call it what you will.

There exists another dimension within this universe. There reside so many souls of those who once walked this earth

Your pathway through life, this life, is merely an opportunity to learn the lessons of life.

The lessons that will help you to understand the necessity to work together; to acknowledge the needs of others; for to do that, others will acknowledge your deeds.

It is a subject upon which I could speak for many, many moons.

My friends beside me will agree, you do acknowledge the need to listen, to learn every day of your earthly existence. You may only do so subconsciously, as you say; your subconscious is perhaps inspired by something deeper within yourselves.

You learn, you speak, and you share your knowledge, your experiences, so others can learn from you.

That perhaps is what you are here for.

Many of your days are happy, others are less so.

Many bring great joys to your lives and you respond to each situation only in a way that you are able through your own experiences.

Each experience strengthens your persona, strengthens your knowledge, and improves your wisdom.

You may ask why some people live lives shorter than others, how are they able to learn so much in such a short time?

They perhaps are more enlightened than others. They perhaps have learned their lessons far quicker than others by having experiences far earlier in their lives than those who live longer, and, in leaving you earlier in their earthly existence they serve others by allowing them to learn, perhaps experience of sadness and grief.

These all add to the growth, the development of the soul.

I often speak of the need for people to work together, to respond to the challenges that exist in your world.

I tire at the times I have urged those who listen, that pray for peace, that pray for help, for those who suffer malnutrition, disease, warfare. Then this desire is shared by all of you here tonight, you, I know, would do all you could to alleviate suffering whenever it occurs.

You are not alone. Many people around your world share your desires. I do not pretend to understand why these things occur when you are so much a part of the majority in your world.

The majority desire peace. The majority desire support for those who are in need. The majority are led by a minority.

Does that not suggest that you are being misled by the minority?

We on our pathways in our lives, do all we can to influence those who are in positions where they can improve the quality of life for impoverished people. We are failing in our mission.

We fail but how can we fail when we draw on resources from your side of life.

Positive resources, positive thoughts. We are unable to draw sufficient thoughts, positive thoughts to overcome the negativity that exists in your world.

The power of negativity is so much stronger than positive thought.

It appears to breed and grow and penetrate the hearts and minds of so many people. It penetrates, dampens the soul, weighs down the mind and suppresses the positive energy.

How can we respond to your desires if your thoughts do not reflect those desires?

It is necessary to believe that you can make a difference, but, there is scepticism amongst you who ask, 'what can I say', 'what can I believe as an individual?'

Do not question, do not hesitate to believe that you can collectively work together to inspire those who need inspiration. You can work together as individuals but collectively believe, trust, inspire, inform.

Then we will draw from your inspiration to add to the efforts to improve the lives of others.

I am being asked to withdraw. I would prefer to continue. I will return, but, I feel a finer mind than mine wishes to communicate. God bless you, I will return.

I became aware of Fine Feather withdrawing and the energy changed to that of a different personality.

Petrah, who had previously spoken began speaking in a much more gentle, refined voice.

Petrah: I wish to speak with you, please allow me to introduce myself. Petrah is my name, Petrah. I spoke to you before, some of you.

I admire your perseverance to listen. Once is a virtue, to listen twice deserves credit, for you have decided for yourselves that communication between myself through this medium is a genuine, believable experience.

For those who are experiencing what you call trance for the first time, may I ask you to listen, learn, question. Decide for yourselves whether you believe that I am from a level of existence that is of a higher mind, shall we say, than yourselves and of Fine Feather.

He will not be pleased to be spoken of in that way. Unfortunately he does still possess a very strong ego. That is ok, as you say, that is acceptable, for he too is still learning to develop.

The desires that we share; the desires to learn the finer things in life... however, I cannot continue on that subject.

There are many people here questioning why they are here, am I right?

Question, you cannot learn without questions. Some will leave this evening as doubtful as you were when you entered this hall.

That is good. Question, but I know you will continue to be inspired to look further than you have. Look deeper into this subject, as you say; this subject of life after death.

Do not fail in you endeavours but question that belief. I can only advise you that I believe; for I am not the dead, am I?

I am speaking from a world you cannot see, you cannot hear, you cannot even acknowledge with your own senses, but I do speak to you. I speak honestly and I hope sincerely.

You have already received some philosophy. Thoughts from someone who wishes to do good.

I could continue along those lines. I could speak of my desires to improve your lives.

I could not add more than was said. It is for you to speak of what we have said, for you to work on your own prayers, your own thoughts, your own positivity.

I can no more add to what Fine Feather has said, therefore I might be inclined to invite you to speak to me. You may wish to challenge what you see, what you hear, what you witness.

You may wish to ask many, many questions.

I will do my best to answer and perhaps persuade you even more that I am from a different level of life. A different existence where I have observed and worked for many, many years, I use your term for time.

Years are your way of measuring your time here upon earth.

We have no time of years, days, we have no acknowledgement of daylight or darkness but I must stop if you wish to speak, please do so'.

Question: Are we encouraged by the Spirit world to do things which normally, if left to our own devices, we would not normally undertake?

Petrah: You are encouraged, you are influenced, and you receive inspiration for your thoughts and deeds. You receive words. You receive thoughts that give you opportunities to respond to your daily experiences. Does that answer your question?

Question: I was told I would be tested by Spirit world concerning things I have lived through. I would like it confirmed.

Petrah: I cannot permit you to believe that we make things happen to you or for you. You must accept your earthly conditions; your earthly connection, your earthly habits, your earthly life experiences.

You are directly responsible for your own experiences. You cannot change things by your attitude to life. We are all given trials, as you say. Trials are problems, use your words.

We are only able to inspire you with books. We cannot change your earthly surroundings. I think you refer to earthly conditions that cause you much grief, cause you to question why you must bear this burden. Why not?

Life is an experience, a learning experience. It is an opportunity for you to grow spiritually, to learn to acknowledge the experiences from others. You share those experiences, you learn from them.

This enables you to help those who in the future suffer the same experience. You become a beacon by inspiration for others to learn from.

Is that not a desirable asset?

Question: I came here to speak to people in your world. I see mediums who speak to people in your world. If I were more open minded, would I be able to speak to people in your world?

Petrah: Open-minded, how you mean? How you say open-minded? In this movement?

In my world we have no religion. Where we are; we believe in God, one God.

We are, as you say, open-minded. We have no desire to instil dogma into your minds.

You are not alone in your religion. Your religion is not the main instrument of your mind.

Your religion is merely a system of belief, the coming together of minds, perhaps.

Open-mindedness is more relevant here, for you have no dogma. You have no attachments.

You merely seek the proof of what we say. Others, other religions, seek no proof of their dogma, their beliefs. Therefore, they perhaps, are less able to absorb that which can open their eyes.

That which can inspire to achieve what they too desire.

Opening minds is something we try to do. Your mediums are merely open-minded, but they have merely progressed beyond the point of belief, of observance and they have opened themselves to the influence of others; the influence of another dimension that many, many people seek to deny.

But many more seek to enquire. Mediums are merely open-minded people and sadly they work in what you call a minority religion.

Your other religions are open to the presence of God, but, they seek to deny the existence of the eternal life. They seek to demand. How can they possibly reconcile their thoughts?

They're curious, they're curious.

Question: How can anybody justify the killing of people in the name of religion?

Petrah: There is no justification. Are you sure their motive is religious?

Are you sure their motive is not greed under the name of religion?

They seek control however they exist. They seek to control the minds of people who do not share their way of life; their attitudes, their teachings.

Is that religion? I think not. You cannot share the views of everybody in your world.

You cannot agree with all that is said and done because you have lived a life within a culture different from others.

Living elsewhere, but, there lies the difference in your thoughts.

But do not confuse religion with desire for control, for power.

Religion means service, serve your fellow men. Do not attempt to indulge your thoughts, impose your thoughts on others, but merely guide them. Share your thoughts, speak truthfully, speak your views, and do not impose.

Your religions seek to question how it can be possible for individuals to believe something different.

Is that not indoctrination; the seeking of power over an individual?

You are an individual, you will continue to be an individual, but therefore you may permit yourself to think, to think for yourselves. Belief, belief is not necessary when you know.

Think for yourselves. Do not blame religion.

Blame the people, the individuals who seek to change the minds of others.

Peace is the ultimate goal, peace is what you all desire, peace can be achieved but do not look towards religion for peace.

Look towards yourselves, your own thoughts, your own way of living.

You can be a beacon for others as an individual.

There are many individuals who have existed, who are revered today, for their light shone.

They influenced people, they inspired people peacefully. They sought not to indoctrinate, they sought only to inspire.

They had many followers but many, many enemies but they were not speaking of religion but of peace.

You know to kill is wrong. You need no label attached to that motive; no label permits you to justify your act. You cannot justify the death of another if you are responsible for that death.

May I take one more question? I must withdraw.

Question: May I ask what era you are from?

Petrah: I was asked before from whence I came. I have only knowledge of a dry, arid, hot climate.

I lived a life of peace within a commune. I was a worker within a monastery. I observed their methods, their lives. I wore a white cloak. I remember there was no desire other than to serve.

We served together for each other.

76

We used the land for food. We prayed in solitude and I had no desire to be a monk, but I chose to serve those who did.

My time on this earth was shorter than your lives, but I am pleased to say, I lived a life of peace; a peace that you can only dream of many, many, many years before you existed on this earth.

I cannot speak more of my earthly existence.

Thank you, I will withdraw, I thank you for your questions. I thank you for your patience.

God bless, goodnight.

Then Fine Feather returned…

Fine Feather: I am fine Feather, you have witnessed a communication with those who reside on my, in your words, my side of life.

You use terms of reference on my side of life but there are no sides. There are only, how you say, adjacent existences. You understand energy; you understand waves of sound, waves of light?

We merely exist within these spheres of life that are no different from that which you cannot see but which you use every day. But yet you accept the existence of waves of sound you cannot accept the existence of what you might call waves of Spirit, waves of energy within which we reside.

I believe some of you are questioning my words.

I apologise, you do accept there is an existence other than this. Many of you do but there are those with whom you speak, cannot accept that which they cannot touch, see, hear, but still are they not the same? Invisible?

Sometimes they accept their senses; they do not accept our position in their lives, very sad.

I feel my time with you must come to an end, I have communicated for many, many years. I have developed myself with others, who are not present tonight.

We have shared many experiences. We have observed things which were deemed to be unlikely to happen, but have happened. I have never spoken of something that I have not believed in.

I have only spoken of something that I felt was of importance. I have never failed to attend when the need arose to give statements, inspiration and support when the need was there.

I shall continue to provide all that I have before, as long as my own medium is prepared to work with me.

I must withdraw.

I must thank you for believing in the dedication of this circle, this church. Believing in what your representatives aspire to. Believing that you can hear the words of those you call Spirit. God bless you all.

Trance Demonstration - 16 January 2010
Croydon Spiritualist Church

My guide Fine Feather spoke for about forty minutes before three other individuals spoke, including our late Vice President, Pat Deverell. Unfortunately the recording was incomplete and the other three individual's words were not recorded.

Fine Feather: Good evening, my name is Fine Feather.

I have a very long acquaintance with my instrument, Alan.

I was introduced to him by another medium and I impressed myself forcefully and spoke to Alan, insisting that he must work with me.

I remember Alan was very hesitant.

However, it is his nature to question and investigate and having made the introduction, his curiosity was aroused and I am pleased he has allowed me to speak to others of the reality of what you call 'the world of Spirit'.

I was expecting to speak to a greater number of people in your church this evening but I understand conditions have been difficult.

(Weather conditions had made travel difficult).

Therefore it is good that those who are here are interested to learn about this world you call 'the world of Spirit'; to learn about the aspect of this religion that you may not have experienced before, and that is good.

For we are on a pathway of many experiences, understandings and I hope you will continue to learn from those who represent your religion.

I am always an instrument, an instrument of communication. I can inform you of how my own life has progressed since I left this world – this Earth Plane as you call it, many, many, many moons ago.

My memory is very faint, however as a result of my continuous attempts to speak through Alan and continuous awareness of the earth life through attending, my memory has improved sufficiently to tell you of my former existence here on earth.

I was what you call an Indian, working on the plains of a country you now call America.

We had no need for names for we believed that we were the only ones and ours was the only land, and therefore our existence was to be at one with nature and the Great Spirit.

Ah, I hear you say, Great Spirit, how did we know the Great Spirit, when you refer in modern times to the Great Spirit?

I answer that we were a very spiritual race and we believed in the power of nature. We believed in the seasons of life, of age, of degeneration, of new life.

And we credited this evolution to what you call, God.

However God, as the Great Spirit, encompasses far more than you can ever know, and through our meditations, our times of peace and quiet and solitude we became aware of those around us, our ancestors who had passed through the door you call death, and we became aware of words of wisdom communicated from these people, and therefore through evolution our minds allowed us to understand where our departed relations existed.

It must be what you call the world of Spirit.

It follows that in that world there must be a greater force of good, a greater force of existence, which is responsible for all we see, hear and touch, and to that, we gave the name Great Spirit.

We were often in communication with those who lived in that world.

We were given advice, warnings, communication of many kinds. When to venture forth; when to remain where we were.

The seasons often changed suddenly and abruptly and we were warned of such events.

We learned to trust, we learned to work together for all, when nobody had too little and nobody had too much.

Our children were our future and therefore we nurtured them to work with us and become responsible adults for the future, and thus, our existence was harmonious; harmonious with each other, harmonious with nature, and harmonious with the Great Spirit.

This trilogy enabled us to live peacefully and have abundance of what nature has given but unfortunately I witnessed after my departure from your world, a great transformation in that which was important for the existence of mankind, and that, my friends was a very heavy burden for me to bear, unable to influence that which was happening; unable to help those who were struggling to maintain their earthly existence, which had been happening for many, many centuries.

That is 'progress' as you call it. To us it was a backward step. Spiritually the world is now barren; barren of ideas and always in need.

Yes, you talk of the need to help those who are suffering wherever they may be.

However I feel that the greater need is of self-protection before helping others.

As a tribe we shared, and as I said, 'no one had too little and no one had too much.'

And yet I see in your world extremes of wealth and extremes of poverty, and much in between of course.

Until these extremes have been abolished, destroyed, the world will continue to have disharmony; disharmony through corruption, through selfishness, through the need to protect things that you have collectively, rather than share and reduce the misery that exists in your world.

But that is not why I am here. I do not wish to make you feel guilty as an individual. I do not wish to make you feel lesser a person than myself. I merely point out that we had a life, an existence where we shared all that the Great Spirit offered, we lost nothing and we lived in harmony.

That should be your aim throughout your life. As you think, so you are and as you are, you have influence by thinking clearly and being what you might call 'a better person.'

Allow others to follow your example. If those who govern you are unable to fulfil the wishes of the people, then those people who govern you are not worthy of your support.

I realise that you are unable to have individual influence upon these events and these people but collectively you can have great power.

You need a leader who understands the needs of the people. You need an influential speaker who can influence those who need leadership.

However, whenever in the past, such a person has appeared, his demise has become almost inevitable.

There have been scholars, religious people, Presidents, Kings, all nature of individuals. They have become a force for good, creating leadership for those who choose a less selfish existence, but they been deemed troublesome.

Can you understand the frustration that we feel when such a person is sent to your world, is nurtured, is taught and learns to understand a better way of living, and then to go forward to speak for the common good, only to be suppressed and in some cases, deceased?

You know what I mean by these words. If they are not imprisoned, their lives are taken from them.

I apologise for speaking as I do, but this is a lesson for you. It seems as speak of my earthly existence, it follows that I could speak of your existence and make a comparison, for you to understand.

It has taken centuries to lose the way we existed of sharing and o brotherhood, to the existence we have now of selfishness and greed.

It will take centuries to turn back the clock I fear, but I find there is c common good among all peoples when they are allowed to think freely and openly. When they are allowed to show the Spirit within themselves, given free rein to express itself.

There are many, many hundreds of thousands of people of like mind, bu where is the leader bold enough to bring together that which is necessary to make your lives more peaceful and equitable now?

Can you understand my disappointment if we are unable to influence a greater number of people other than those within this church tonight?

One day my friends, the breakthrough will happen.

People such as myself will influence others around your world in such numbers that you will find a natural leader to take you forward, to unite people in a common good; taking away the artificial props of power tha your governments built around them.

It has happened before in a small way, it can happen again.

Whenever there are natural disasters in your world there is a grea outpouring of peace, love and harmony in wishing to help.

A great outpouring of unselfish thought.

Why do you need a natural disaster for such a powerful emotion to appear? Why, why, why?

The power of Spirit is there for you to use. But you must wish to use it to make a difference, for things to change.

I shall leave these thoughts with you, and I shall return to speak with you after others have spoken with you this evening.

Once again there was a break in the recording and further communication was not recorded.

82

Trance Demonstration - January 2011
Croydon Spiritualist Church

Mollie, recognising that Fine Feather was with us greeted him before he began speaking, saying, good evening Fine Feather, how are you?

Fine Feather: I am well, it is a pleasure for me to be here and I am never more pleased than to work within your church.

It is always a source of amusement to me that my friend Alan is nervous of such an event, wondering 'will I be here with him?'

Am I ever far from him?

I am far more of an influence upon his life than he gives me credit for. However, that is as it shall be. Now I greet you all within this church.

Good Evening, I am very pleased that you have chosen to be here this evening, and I am hopeful that you will all learn something of benefit this evening.

I have spoken to many within this church before, sometimes when Alan has least expected me to be here, with a prepared speech.

(When preparing to take a service within the church, I will usually have a subject on which to speak, but it has been known for me to stand up and unexpectedly be taken over by Fine Feather who will then take over the speaker's role).

I cannot always allow him that privilege. Sometimes I feel what I have to say is more beneficial to the congregation of this church and therefore, I override his thoughts and his feelings, and now as I feel stronger, as usual, I begin to shake and I cannot prevent myself from using the energy in this way.

Please apologise to Alan when I have finished.

And now as I am here I shall share some thoughts with you; some thoughts about your religion, your world, and my world which you call the Spirit world.

It should come as no surprise to you, those who are here, that my world and your world are not separate worlds.

Indeed they inter- penetrate to such an extent that we are one, and we are able to communicate with you and through the mediums who work within this church and others around your world.

It is our privilege to be able to confirm that we exist within what you call the world of Spirit.

We are purely Spirit with consciousness, understanding, beliefs; all what you might call abstract attributes, for we are not of solid form, as you can see 'solid form'.

It has been said by many within this church that other religions understand that there is a life after your physical death. They speak of the holy spirit, the holy ghost, they speak of a life hereafter, but, in what you call 'Spiritualism' where you prove that we exist, I correct myself, we prove that we exist, suddenly your other religions close down.

I cannot understand their mode of thinking. I cannot understand their denial of a hope of meeting those who have gone before in our world when they depart this world.

Why do they fear and instil fear in the believers of their faith?

It is often said that fear is the greatest trait of mankind.

We fear so many things for which we have no need to fear. I for one when I communicate, never encourage you to fear anything from the world of Spirit. I come in friendship; I come to enable you to understand that we who are with you at all times can help to enable you to surpass the expectations of your own beliefs.

If we can encourage you to understand that you are more than a physical being with a brain, if we can help you to understand that your mind and your consciousness separates at physical death, as if you are in a dream state, and that you can look forward to a continuous existence, an existence that I cannot begin to explain to you.

I've heard it spoken that there are colours, there is music, there is a natural landscape that is beyond compare with what you see around you.

What you see around you is of God.

It is beautiful, it is creative, it is inspiring, you become aware of the world of Spirit. Your senses will be reawakened to a stronger even more beautiful inspired surroundings.

My heart, I cannot speak of a physical heart, but my emotional heart yearns for the people of this world to understand what I am saying. Your world has many troubles. Your world has many people who choose to destroy, to damage, to hurt, even to take life.

These people are misguided and the guidance they receive is from other misguided souls, those who seek power for themselves, but for no noble cause, those who seek power over weaker souls; whose influence is far stronger than other minds. Those they overpower.

Then they abuse the power they have, and they are a very small minority in your world and yet by force they demand, they are revered by those who are subservient to them.

My friends this is a state of affairs that cannot be allowed to continue.

As more and more people are destroyed they come to our world confused, utterly confused and it is for us to help them to understand that in the world of Spirit, the power of good has overcome the power of which you call evil.

That is not to say that there are no people of bad mind in our world.

Of course there are.

As you are before you leave your physical world you shall be when you arrive in the world of Spirit. Your reality, your traits, your beliefs do not change, within the seconds of time of physical to Spiritual life and therefore it is true that in the world of Spirit we have what you call levels of existence.

There are many words to describe these levels, these planes of existence if you will, but as you experience in your world, like does attract like.

Those who enjoy a particular pastime will share their enjoyment with those of a like mind and those who mix with people who wish to damage the environment or have power over people, will join together in like mind and they in turn do not change as they pass through the veil we call death.

I have spoken of the light within our world. I suggest to you that it is your light that enables us to work for the common good. Your light enables us to see the darkness, to create a shadow in the world of spirit. Creating shadows surrounding those who live in the darkness, those who will cause trouble, and then we are able to separate from the less enlightened entities in our world, energy of good and peace and light, to enable them to see a good light to see a better way to live.

That is what we do.

We attempt to bring our influence to bear on those people in your world who are the cause of much strife and turmoil but without the help of people such as my friends Mollie and Patricia. Without their help and others all around your world, the light does not shine and therefore it is more difficult for us to penetrate the darkness surrounding the people who create the turmoil.

It must be very difficult for you to accept my words as fact, but I urge you to use your own minds. Question what you are told. I have told you I once was the same as you.

I lived amongst the plains of a distant land. I questioned what I was told by my elders, but I lived according to the rules of that time, close to nature and nature was our greatest guide.

We learnt that as you did to the world around you, to the people around you, so you would receive in equal measure for I have progressed for the many ages that I have been in the world of Spirit.

I have learned so much that I cannot question the validity of those words, 'as you speak of others, as you think of others, as you do to others there is a reflection that will bring those thoughts, those words, those deeds back to you and your consciousness'.

It will be stored within you until such time that you understand that you now need to absolve yourself of the thoughts and the deeds and the words that harm others, for you are being harmed by actions.

I was not aware of such a thing when I lived in your world.

Throughout my life I rebelled, I fought, and I have to tell you I killed to survive and that brings me to motive.

The Great Spirit, God as we call him, provides us with all that we need with which to exist, and there were times in desperation in my life when it was necessary to take the life of an animal to survive, for the fur, for the food, even for the skeletal remains to create tools and weapons, for we too were under threat from other people in our environment.

It was necessary to create tools and weapons with which to defend ourselves and therefore motive was a very, very strong influence upon the way we lived and it is not until my life was threatened that I learnt to understand the interconnectivity between individuals and nature, and gradually I became wiser and more understanding of what was to be.

The circumstances of your lives are so much different. You are governed rather than to work for yourselves. You are governed and dare I say, you are told what to think.

You are told what to believe, you are told how to live your lives and if you choose to speak against what you are told, I think I am right in suggesting that your lives will be made difficult.

Those who govern you will tend to suppress the thoughts that you have.

You may consider that your thoughts are of a minority, but may I suggest that you are not of a minority?

You are peace loving. You wish to be at one with nature, you wish there will be no hunger, you wish that everybody could be at the same standard of living and yet, and yet, it is not to be.

How can you not see that the inequitable world in which you live is a source of much anger and antagonism around your world?

There are those who rebel against the society in which they live, the governments that control their lives.

There are those who are losing their lives for their beliefs, but still there are more of the same beliefs who choose to continue the struggle for an equitable life.

I believe I am right when I say there are those within this church this evening, who share the suffering that these people endure. They share the suffering, they send out thoughts of love and healing to those people who are less fortunate than themselves and that, my friends is what religion is about.

Religion is not purely worshipping God.

I use the word God. I mean one God. There are hundreds of religions and beliefs in your world.

There is only one God, only one God.

His energy, His power interpenetrates every nation every individual, every plant, every animal, for they are all of his creation.

They are all created with love and peace and with harmony, but where is the harmony in your world and what has caused it to disappear?

Mankind, mankind with free will has generated factions that disagree over relatively minor issues.

It is the leaders of those factions that generate greater harm, hate, dislike, and disharmony.

It is not the people.

The great mass of people who fill your world cry out for peace and even though you have more than you need, there are those that have so little.

It has taken many, many centuries for your world to create the situation that exists in your world.

I suggest it is not very long since the disharmony, differences of opinion have generally become so great, the more your world has become aware of other nations.

Does that make sense?

Because your world is now known to everybody, every part of your world, every life, every country, is known. It has become more unequal because of interference from one nation to another.

A more powerful nation has influenced a smaller nation against its will and therefore disharmony has been created and I suggest that over the entire world there are many, many situations where smaller, less influential parts of your world have been taken in the grip of a stronger force, creating disharmony.

Centuries ago of course there were wars. There were battles, but other parts of the world were allowed to live their lives according to their own traditions and origins.

It is as in the world that I came from, when other countries invaded our country, the harmony was broken.

That has continued and accelerated and it has not been challenged.

I ask you to think within yourselves, 'is that the life you wish to have around you?'

It is our chosen vocation to try to influence those around your world to accept that these things cannot be allowed to continue. Each person that passes to our world suffers due to the teaching they received in your world and our work is multiplied.

It is for us to try to create a situation in your world where people understand the way their lives are led. With them it is within their personality.

If they can be taught within your world that peace harmony, goodwill is a better way, then the task we have is greatly reduced. There is warfare where thousands of people are killed in a matter of hours.

The work we have to do when they pass to the world of Spirit!!

We have an army of people in what you call Spirit; working to enable these people to understand that they are no longer in their physical bodies and we teach them that their new surroundings are no longer the same as their old ones.

A very difficult task, except when those who have passed understood before they left your world that there was continuity of the Spirit, of the soul, of the mind, of the consciousness that you wish to choose and they continue to work with us from our side of life, to create harmony and peace where they can.

I can go on and on, on this subject I could repeat my words. I could change my words. I could give the same meaning to you, but I feel I have made the point I came to make.

I wish that each one of you will be able to depart this church this evening and take with you the words that you have heard to influence others for the good of mankind, but I understand that when you leave here and you tell a friend, a colleague, a member of your family who has no belief such as yours, you may be ridiculed.

You have heard words from a man who is in the world of Spirit, who lived thousands of years ago I know that you will be thinking that you will be ridiculed.

How many would it take?

88

How many of you would it take to pass on these words to so many others before there is a greater interest in the words that are used?

If one man can stand before a thousand people and speak as I have done and when I say one man, I mean a man who exists in your physical world, he can influence a thousand people and at least half of those people go forward and repeat his words, why cannot it be possible that a man such as myself speaking to you cannot have the same influence?

I suggest that it is because of the existence of your religions, your sects, your organisations.

They cannot accept that we are able to communicate with you.

Knowledge brings responsibility and I accept my responsibility to speak when I can.

When I am able I speak the truth of the continuous existence of your soul, your Spirit.

Those here, who work for the good of this church, passing on these words and these thoughts and the thoughts of people who have spoken before, you have Silver Birch, who has written and spoken words and they have been transferred into the written word.

A great influence in your world, that is to say those who have chosen to read his words.

My friends how much more beneficial would this be if these words were repeated beyond this church, beyond this area, beyond your shores?

How much more beneficial will they be to people compared to the books that are quoted every week and every year for centuries?

Words that have little meaning in the minds of people who listen, books claiming to represent the son of God.

Some are very fine words, many are confusing, and to some there is no understanding of what is meant by them.

Visions of your world are the cause of so much misunderstanding and conflict and until they are challenged, conflicts will continue.

Visions of Spiritualism had a beginning much longer ago than your acknowledgement of it.

It had a beginning many, many centuries ago, stories were arranged to enable those in power to have control and this is why there is inequality and conflict in your world.

A mighty challenge has been set before us to change, what we know cannot be allowed to continue if you wish to live in a peaceful world, but a challenge exists.

The more and more people learn to understand the truth of the Spirit; the influence will progress from man to man, town to town, country to country. Until such time that we have achieved our cause.

I feel I have spoken enough, I shall withdraw but I shall return and as usual there are others here who may wish to make their presence known.

Be assured that you are protected by people around us in my world and no person of bad intent will be permitted to come to your church.

Many, who have seen your light, are drawn to the light in this church. It is a light of love and peace and that is how they present themselves to me and they bring their love and their peace to you individually and collectively.

I shall allow them to take my place and speak to you as they wish.

God bless you.

Once again there was a break in the recording and further communication was not recorded.

Trance Demonstration - January 2012
Croydon Spiritualist Church

Fine Feather: Greetings I am Fine Feather, it is very humbling to be with you this evening.

I have looked forward to this opportunity to speak with you all, however it is necessary for me to entrance my medium a little more before I can say that which I wish to say.

I have attempted to quieten my mediums mind and have succeeded to a great extent; however there are many things that he himself wishes to say that I must not permit him to say.

This is an opportunity for me to express my thoughts and feelings upon the lives that you live, and if I allow Alan to interject his own thoughts, then mine will be stilted.

Therefore bear with me as I speak of little interest for a while.

It is an accomplishment for me to speak within your church and a privilege I might add.

There are many who would benefit from my thoughts but it is sufficient that those who are here listen and then question what they are about to witness and that is my intention.

It is many, many moons since I spoke within your church and that is something I regret, however your earthly lives are very busy and therefore I understand that I must be patient and make myself even more understood on the rare occasions that I am able to speak.

You have been very helpful in your endeavours to free the souls of those who have passed to my world but have not understood their new environment, and therefore the fear they had of what you call death instilled by their indoctrination, would not permit them to move towards the light of the Spirit world.

Therefore they hid in the darkness between this world and the next and you will know that you have freed many people from such a condition. The light that you have shed has created the shadow of the person that was lost in time and space that we have interceded to free them, enlighten them, and bring them to those they have lost prior to their own transition.

91

The love that they found was sufficient to encourage them to move with me and friends into the world of Spirit.

That, my friends is one of the many, many missions that you enlightened souls can add, with your efforts to help those who not only have not made the full transition those but those who live in ignorance of what you call 'the next life' in the world of what you call Spirit.

Because of ancient teachings that continue to this day, there is much strife and fear, intimidation, antagonism, warfare, in the name of God. The fear that has indoctrinated so many for many, many centuries is still inherent in the minds of people this day.

Fear of death. Supposition that there is only heaven and hell. The supposition that there may only be darkness. The supposition that when your earthly life is terminated by whatever means, there is nothing to expect but damnation and punishment.

Friends I hope that you are sufficiently enlightened by what you have experienced within this church over time that you understand that there is nothing to fear, nothing.

Death is merely a transition from a physical world to what you might describe as a non-material world. A world that is governed by thought. A world that is governed by your own mental energy, your consciousness, call it what you will.

I am therefore I am. I am nothing but myself.

I have become more aware of myself since my transition to my world from your world many, many years ago.

In your world my life was what you would call, about survival.

Living one day to the next, necessitating hunting for food, feeding not only my family but my neighbours, my friends with whom I lived.

We worked together for common good. If one had little and others had more in abundance, the goods were shared, the food was shared.

The clothing that we made from the skins of animals was shared. Women toiled to produce that which man needed for hunting, was shared without thought, without hostility. Nothing was taken. All was given and therefore at my transition I was not as surprised at what I found in the next life because my whole being was based upon the continuous life awaiting me.

We worshipped God the Great Spirit.

We worshipped, we worshipped in a physical way.

We energised ourselves on the surroundings that we had, from the wind and the soil, the shifting sands. The wind was the energy we worshipped, for in our primitive way we understood that the wind was of the Great Spirit. Not physical, but a form that you call energy that had an influence upon our lives.

That was our primitive interpretation of the Great Spirit, the maker of all life, the great creator of all that had been created in our environment. We understood that all that had been created was available for all to share, for all to share equally, my friends.

I ask you to turn your thoughts to the nature of my physical life to the nature of the environment in which you live.

Do you share all that you have?

Is there nobody in your world without food, without water, without shelter?

Do you find that the surpluses of the minerals and the wealth in your world, are shared so that no one has too little?

I think we all know the answer to that, and I am saddened at what I see in your modern world.

It may be modern but friends it is not equitable and as I have observed for many, many years from my primitive life, there has been progress in so many ways for the benefit of mankind.

It is good progress, but the progress has not been shared in such a way that all have benefited equally.

I was one of the first to witness the effect of man's inhumanity to man when my lands were overrun by those who appeared on our shores; from where, we knew not.

They appeared peacefully at first, and then changed to greed, avarice what you call human nature.

The land of my father, my ancestors, progressively was destroyed by other men, then aggressively taken for granted.

In your world there was very great material change in the mind of man, a material change that we had never, ever experienced in our simple ways.

Our lack of understanding weakened us for we trusted those as we trusted ourselves, each other.

Trust is very easily broken.

I cannot say to you that all progress has been bad but I do say to you that with all that you have in your world so much more could be done to improve

93

the lives of everybody. This I have spoken of many times before and I cannot continue to speak in the same way.

I find, though you listen, you are few and the possibilities that you have to influence those who have great power in your world are few. And therefore it is left for us in the world of Spirit to generate conditions that help to influence those who dominate your world, and I use the word dominate, for that is what they do.

The few govern the majority because the majority are weakened by the structures established by the minority to prevent protest.

It is now for us to attempt to influence your world from our side of life. Let it be known that you are not alone in your thoughts and your prayers that you send to your loved ones in the world of Spirit.

You are not alone.

Whoever prays to God through whatever religious structure you use, those prayers are received if sent sincerely, and those prayers and those thoughts of love and healing are sent to us.

There is no dogma attached, no religious connection once they are heard in our world. They are just sincere thoughts and prayers my friends, they form the energy that we need to work with and for you for the benefit of all.

When the hierarchy struggle to make something work that is not desirable for all mankind, the people in the world of Spirit are preventing the smooth action leaders desire.

Understand that we do have influence on your world and influence is stronger the more people pray to us, to God, the Great Spirit, whatever term you use.

There are many, many things in your world that are not progressing according to the plans of politicians. They have solved a problem then they discover yet more problems. They are never free of problems.

My friends I tell you, this is because they are not seeing what they must do is to benefit all.

They are not, as you would say, connected to the influence of the Great Spirit.

Yes, they attend their religious services. They attend grand ceremonies, pray. They sing, they preach but they are not making their own personal link with the world of Spirit.

They are merely following the dogma of past generations.

Because it was deemed to be right then, it is deemed to be right now.

Where has their power of personal thought disappeared to when they follow this way of life?

Many impositions of power in your religions are aware of what I am saying.

They are open to the influence of Spirit. They know that they can do much good if only they were allowed to. My friends you will know that when one of your souls speaks against the traditional way of thinking, the traditional way of their religion, if they question anything that is said, then they will in turn be demoted, ignored, maybe even made to leave their religion.

And as I speak there are those who lead your religions, making their personal connection to the world of Spirit. They pray for things that you pray for. They ask for equality, for peace for all.

They are heard, but because they cannot shake away the binds of their dogma, their prayers and their thoughts lack sincerity and therefore, the energy generated by them is greatly reduced.

You have people upon your world who work for the world of Spirit. I do not mean those who attach themselves to your religion. I speak of individuals in far away countries who are persecuted for beliefs. Who protest peacefully and spend much of their own time in confinement imposed by those who lead the country in which they live.

But their energy is far greater than the collective energy within the temples the cathedrals the churches all over your world that lack sincerity.

The power of one man or one woman working sincerely and positively for the world of Spirit having no interest in the material things in life, having no need for the material things in life - their power is a thousand fold. A thousand fold greater than those within the collective religion.

I say things that you find hard to understand or believe. I only ask you to think for yourselves. Have your doubts, have your questions, but allow your own thoughts and feelings within to answer the doubts that you have.

You will not be expected to speak in public of what you know before a sceptical audience but you can be expected to speak to your friends and families. You can be expected to support those within churches such as these, where the free thinking Spirit is allowed to express itself.

By supporting them, their influence can grow. Obstacles will always be presented to you, but a continuation of a progressive, honesty, integrity, will eventually break down the barriers that are presented before you.

For truth cannot be questioned. The truth is the truth. It is the truth, nothing else. There is nothing that can destroy the truth.

When people have faith they are constantly questioning their faith.

When people have truth they have little to question because the truth has always withstood comparisons with indoctrination.

But those who speak the truth are respected for their views; respected for the fact that they are able to express themselves without ever deviating from the truth. For that which you said many months ago, when you are asked to speak of the same subject you will say the same things without hesitation because there is nothing to remember, nothing to think about.

You know the truth, and therefore you speak the same truth every time you speak on the subject.

So many unanswered questions; so many fears in the minds of people.

I ask you to delve deeper within yourselves, to study, to listen and then to speak naturally without embellishment. To speak what you feel is comfortable within yourselves, for your intuition is possibly the best guide that you will ever have, because your intuition, when alerted to the presence and influence from the Spirit world, is the greatest thing that you possess.

For emotions generate many, many thoughts and many bad thoughts. Your emotions are moving from one side to the other. Your emotions cause you to worry about many things that you find in your lives, many things that upset you, including the passing of a loved one; including people who will not conform to life within your world.

People whose lives appear to be entirely to do negative things, destructive things, hurtful things. These people generate so much within you that prevents you from thinking purely through your intuitive level.

They destroy peacefulness, they anger you. There are so many emotions that are expressed as a result of the negative influences of those who seek to damage, hurt, create pain for individuals.

Friends, I have to reiterate, if the way of life that you have in this world has generated such people, there are people that have things in abundance people who show no compassion to others; is it not right that you will expect others to be angry at those people, to rebel against a society that supports those people?

It is not for me to justify any of these actions I merely ask you to think of what you call 'cause and effect'.

Everybody was able to understand that what you do to one, you do to yourself.

How much better would your world be, how much better would it be to send out thoughts of love to those who are causing the problems in your life? I say thoughts of love to those... may I correct myself?

The thoughts that you send in your prayers sincerely to those of us in the world of Spirit can be used to influence those who disrupt your lives. I feel that within your own consciousness, your own minds, there is such a natural feeling in yourselves. It is seen that it is natural to react negatively to negative influences.

I speak of revenge, I speak of thoughts that suggest that you would like perhaps, something nasty to happen to somebody who has upset you, but again I speak to you with influence of the world of Spirit.

The world of Spirit is made purely of thought transference.

You have no physical body. Your existence is consciousness.

I cannot force you to understand something you have not experienced, however as you think, so you are. As you think, so you shall become and I know that within your churches, within this church, it is said your thoughts are living things, and therefore can you not see that as your negative thoughts are sent to those to whom they are sent, they will return to you in a negative form?

Much within the human consciousness that is difficult to understand. Thoughts that exist in the minds of your people today are far more negative than has ever been the case.

I need to ask you to trust your prayers, your sincere positive prayers, trust when I say that they are acted upon. Instead of sending a negative thought to a fellow citizen, your brothers, send a positive thought to the world of Spirit and think of the person you wish to influence as you send that thought. We assure you that the singularity and liberty within that person will be reduced.

I sense some doubt within your minds but I cannot explain myself in any other way.

I think in your scientific terms and I delve deep into the mind of my instrument here.

In your science you have negative and you have positive. If you have two of the same, positivity, but if you have one of each there is negativity.

That is for you to decide.

I am in danger of repeating myself should I continue.

Therefore I shall withdraw for a while I feel there are others wishing to speak.

I feel very much love coming to me from this church, much emotion.

I feel within my aura in the Spirit world there are those who may wish to make their presence known. Therefore I shall withdraw, allow others to communicate whatever way they wish to speak and I assure you all that there is no danger.

97

Nothing to fear from the world of Spirit, for around my aura and around this church there are many, many hundreds of people in my world protecting and supporting you in all you do and we will never ever allow anything detrimental to happen within these walls.

God bless you all.

The next person to introduce himself was the docker, Jack who had previously spoken at a trance demonstration.

Jack: ...anybody here?

Mollie: Yes, we're here.

Jack: Mucking about them people in their circles saying, anybody there?

We do laugh, we do laugh 'cause we're there. They keep on switching on their light, switching off their lights can't help noticing they don't do it right.

Mollie: What are they supposed to do?

Jack: What you do. You sit quietly, you have love within yourselves. People sit in their circles in their homes, they talk, laugh. Don't take it seriously. They sit there, 'anybody there?'

We can't work with them, can't work with them at all. They just cause us trouble and we have to sort it out afterwards.

Mollie: What have you been doing, just hopping around circles?

Jack: I keep talking with this Fine Feather bloke. He didn't want me to talk tonight. I thought, I'm not having that, he has to talk don't he?

He has to talk. He wants to tell you how to live your lives, do this, do that. Think about this and that. He does it to me all the time. He is so enlightened, that bloke. He comes from somewhere higher up. He comes down, he talks to us as though we are supposed to understand what he is saying.

I haven't been educated. I don't know half the words he uses so how do I understand what he is saying? Do this, do that.

Anyway I'm happy where I am. I don't want to go anywhere else. Been here, like it here, like coming back to see you lot, 'cause you have a nice way about you. You are a good lot. You work with us, but they won't let me work with you.

I keep getting sent to people like them people saying 'anybody there', and they ask me to muck about with them and have a bit of a laugh.

I don't mind it but they won't let me join you.

Mollie: What do you do?

Jack: We make things move, make noises. We have got rules. if that is something you want you are working sincerely............ that's a big word. They say we are mischievous, we frighten the life out of them. I have been told to go in there and sort it out.

Mollie: Who told you that?

Jack: My mates do it. We used to be like that, me and my mates. It made the day go quicker. Anyway why can't we have some fun with you people?

Mollie: We like a bit of a laugh in this church.

Jack: Don't want to frighten you, the thing is he might have gone, but he is there. I wanted to come through and talk to you. You have so much light and energy you strengthen him against me.

A lot of stuff is their imagination they want things to happen. You do a lot of good stuff here.

Mollie: What else do you do?

Jack: We just are. When I come here it is bright. Where I am, there is not a lot of colour.*

You have to earn your colours.

Mollie: Is that because you are on a lower plane, Fine Feather likes you to listen to him and wants you to progress?

Jack: You are clever, you lot.

Mollie: Maybe you should listen to him?

Jack: You talk a lot of sense. You talk so naturally. I can't talk like that Fine Feather, he keeps on like a great grandfather.... got to do this, got to do that.*

Mollie: He has a lot of wisdom, Jack.

Jack: My Mary has gone. I don't see her anymore, she's gone, she seemed to be getting airy fairy with her words, and now she has gone.

Mollie: Get educated and then you can go with her.

Jack: Can I come back to see you if I learn?

Mollie: Yes.

Jack: You know what he has gone and done? He has done this deliberately because I don't listen to him he is making me listen to you, and I can understand what you're saying.

Mollie: We talk a lot of sense me and Pat. Do you see him when you leave here?

Jack: No, just see light with him, just light. Like a power. You feel him he is so strong this bloke. You get into his aura. Anyway, you get into it and feel energy with him. Not like where you are...shake and talk.

Mollie: Are you a bit frightened of him?

Jack: No just in awe of him, it is just love. I have got to go.

Mollie: You must show, Jack that you are willing to learn. It proves, Jack that you do not know all when we pass.

Jack: No I did not know I got here until I got here. I wasn't here, I was somewhere else. I was talking to people and they were ignoring me.

Mollie: Well, you did not know you had passed?

Jack: Suddenly realised I was not there anymore. I was here.

Mollie: If you get educated you could be very good in coming back and talking to us.

Jack: Miss my Mary, if she has gone further up I'll look out for her. You have made me realise that I cannot keep mucking about with people...anybody there?!

Mollie: You have taught us something tonight. When we get to Spirit world we still have to learn. Next time you come back let us know you have learnt something.

Jack: Are you doing this again one day?

Mollie: Oh yes, goodbye.

Jack: Nice talking to you. God bless you.

Spirit: ... speaking in a very pompous but very educated voice and lightly confused.

Good evening, is it evening? I was expecting to give a lecture. Where is everybody in this room? I was sent here.

Mollie: Who sent you?

Spirit: It was a thought, go to this room, you need to speak. There is much you can learn on my subject. I taught the sciences. I speak of scientific effects of atoms.

Mollie: It might be a bit difficult for us to understand.

Spirit: (by now a little bit impatient): That is why I am here. I am a teacher and that is what I do. I teach people who wish to know about atoms.

Mollie: You will not find many here tonight that want to know about atoms.

Spirit: Why am I here then?

Mollie: What is your name?

Spirit: Professor Archibald Roberts, and this is different.   It was a university.

Mollie: This is not a university, It's a church.

Archibald: Are you aware that science has no affinity with religion? You are aware, so why am I in this church? I cannot begin to make you understand…………

Mollie: Archie, Spiritualism is a science.

Archibald: What is Spiritualism? Never heard of it.

Mollie: We prove that when people pass over, they can come back and communicate, which you are doing.

Archibald: I am not. There is no such thing as a science of Spiritualism.

Mollie: You are, at the moment speaking through a person who is here on earth, and you are in the Spirit world.

Archibald: That is not possible. I should be in a lecture hall. Who brought me here? I have talked about science all my life and never, ever have I come across the science of Spiritualism… not even a religion!

Mollie: When did you die, what year, and who was on the throne?

Archibald: I am not dead, I am talking to you. I have been lecturing on science at a university in London. You are asking me irrelevant questions. What year? Who is on the throne? If you don't know, why ask me? There was Queen Victoria. She supported what I did. I spoke to her on occasions. One of her sons was a student of mine. However, he has since left and I have heard nothing of him. Now, can I continue with my lectures but not in this church?

Mollie: Shall we send you somewhere where you can you see a light? Look around.

Archibald: Candlelight?

Pat: A small light, go towards the light.

Archibald: (in a very indignant voice) Are you telling me what to do madam… ?

Pat: Oh blimey, you are in the wrong place, and we want to get you to the right place Archibald.

Archibald: Archibald!? Professor to you!

Pat: If you walk towards the light, you will go to your halls of learning and deliver your lecture.

Archibald: I have never been spoken to in such a way by a woman. You are telling me what I should do!

Pat: No we are advising you.

Archibald: I think I shall leave you anyway. This is not for me. I wish you well with your... Spiritualism. Good luck to you!

The following may be coincidence or wishful thinking but you, the reader are free to draw your own conclusions. Although the surname of Roberts was given, it is often the case that, as the last three letters of Robertson are 'soft', that the name was misheard or 'Archibald' himself didn't give his correct name due to the time lapse between his passing and his return to our event.

We found a Dr. Archibald Robertson, (Right Reverend) who was Vice Chancellor of the London University between 1902 and 1903. (29 June 1853 – 29 January 1931) was the seventh Principal of King's College London who later served as Bishop of Exeter. He was born in Sywell, and educated at Bradfield College and Trinity College, Oxford where he graduated with a first class degree in Classics. He went on to serve as Principal of King's College London from 1897 to 1903, and received an honorary doctorate (LL.D) from the University of Glasgow in June 1901.

He was elected Bishop of Exeter in 1903, serving until 1916.

His son, of the same name, was the communist and atheist Archibald Robertson (atheist) (1886-1961). (Source – Wikipedia).

Greetings.

Mollie: You're back Fine Feather?

Fine Feather: I am with you once again, and I am grateful for your energy. Your energy has enlightened my friends who have attended. Your friend, your Jack he is very stubborn. His life revolves around flippancy and I have told him it is time for him to become more enlightened than he is.

You remember when he first attended this church, he was not aware of his situation and environment and you enlightened him as to his new life?

It is time for him to progress to a more enlightened phase of his progress and that is why his wife Mary was encouraged to progress before Jack. Now he will progress with the help you have given him. He will return to speak to you on future occasions.

Your other friend very, very difficult, very difficult for me to penetrate. A very logical and intelligent mind is preventing him from understanding that he is no longer enlightened.

To those he taught, giving his lectures, as you call it, on a subject that has been...I will use the word indoctrinated...into him. He cannot think differently from that which he was taught, and every effort we make to enlighten him to his new environment is rejected by his logical mind.

To him it is illogical that he has died. He says, 'how can I be dead if I can still communicate with people?'

We try to explain the science that he had taught to him by others, denies him the opportunity to open his mind and expand his consciousness which is not of your world.

Even tonight you have been unable to enable him to understand the error of his mind.

I feel I must stop speaking to you but I shall give you the opportunity to question before I depart.

Anybody who wishes to be enlightened beyond which I have spoken this evening, I feel the questions will appear in your minds after you have left this church.

Question: Does the professor know he has passed?

Fine Feather: He realises something has happened but the logic of his mind is impenetrable. He no longer exists in the material world.

The knowledge he has is of no use to anybody else.

It is a very long process for someone who has for so long been indoctrinated in one subject and he is used to being respected; looked up to, whatever way you speak…… and he cannot accept that there are those above him in knowledge and understanding.

But he will, he will.

Question: Many of us who have lost loved ones, wait and wait for messages. Sometimes we get a message, sometimes we do not.

When they pass do they know they can communicate or do they have to be shown?

Fine Feather: My friend, it is entirely dependent upon their own open mindedness. If they have attended what you call a Spiritualist church, they will at least have understood that communication exists even if they have not received communication for themselves, and therefore their minds will be open to the prospect of communicating with their loved ones when they enter the next life.

Those who are blind to the possibility, to communication will be enlightened as to the error of their ways. They will not be told, they will discover for themselves when they are ready to open themselves the understanding of the Spirit world and their part in it.

We do not educate, we enlighten.

Question: There must be people who do not want to communicate?

103

Fine Feather: The professor is one case. In fact there are those who wish not to communicate. They immediately busy themselves, learning and understanding. Therefore their thoughts do not enter the realms, the aura of your churches.

However if a specific thought from your world is directed towards them, then they will receive that thought and may choose to react to it.

I give you my sincere thanks for allowing me to speak to you in your church.

I do hope that you have understood my words.

I hope even more that you will be able to act upon them for the benefit of those whose lives you touch.

God bless you all.

Trance Demonstration - February 2013

Croydon Spiritualist Church

Once again Fine Feather was eager to speak to his congregation and immediately started speaking.

Greetings, I am Fine Feather, it is a pleasure for me to be allowed to speak to you this day. I am grateful for the opportunity to speak to you.

I am very interested, I am curious to understand the inability for many in your world to understand the existence of the world you call 'Spirit'.

I cannot comprehend the reasons why you are doubtful that we can communicate, we can give evidence and we can provide energy for healing for the betterment of those who are in need.

Why, when there is so much evidence around you and about you within your world of the existence of those who once lived among you.

There is a consciousness through which we are able to communicate.

There is a widespread belief in your world, throughout your world, that purports to believe that there is a further existence after physical death.

The majority of the people in your world speak of a life hereafter.

They speak of being in a better place when they have lost a friend or relation and yet, and yet, there is still resistance to an acknowledgement that we and others are able to communicate.

I am frustrated and saddened that I am aware around me in my spiritual existence, there are many, many people unable to assure their loved ones many of whom are lonely and are unable to communicate with them because those left behind are fearful of the consequences of accepting that they may be able to communicate with those who have gone before.

How very sad.

Your world is in desperate need of love, of peace and of harmony and my world has all in abundance. In abundance!

If we were permitted to communicate to those who have positions of power, many holding those positions merely for prestige, if we were allowed to communicate our message of peace, love and harmony, co-existence with our brothers and sisters, we could surely improve the lives of the many, many people who are suffering from hunger, from fear, disease.

105

I need not continue with those words for you are very aware of that which I speak.

You, by your presence here, are aware that there is a world that you will one day inhabit, and I suggest that you too, will wish to communicate with those whom you have loved. Those who mourn for you, those who yearn to hear your voice, to know that you are aware, and they are aware of continuous progression in your lives.

The additions to the families, the growth of the children, the prospects of those who are related.

Do you not think that because those loved ones have passed to our world, do you not think that they are still mentally connected consciously to those they love?

Are you not saddened by the knowledge that there is fear among peoples, fear instilled by your religions, that it is wrong to communicate with those who have passed?

My friends, we are not dead.

Death is a word that describes the physical decay of your body that has come to the end of its earthly existence. It is a word, nothing more.

However I must tell you that I am alive. Do you agree?

General agreement from those present.

Do I sound as if I am dead?

Of course not. So death is a word, life is continuous. It is more than a word. It is a word that describes all that has gone before and all that will continue into eternity, and my friends, I am still in awe of that which I see, that which I am aware of and that which is yet to come.

Like you I am unaware of our future existence, but I am aware that there will be an existence for me in the future.

Life is merely progression from one state to another, one position to another. It begins from conception, progresses to birth, and a child, in its innocence is still aware of the people in what you call the world of Spirit.

He communicates with those of a similar nature, of a similar disposition as his own.

He befriends them, plays with them until your education tends to break the link the child has.

That is not necessarily detrimental to the child. His childhood is important for his development and his own physical progress.

However as he develops and learns, becomes knowledgeable and becomes a thinking person he will begin to question as I am sure the children you have borne have done.

There are many, many questions they ask.

'Where are they from?' 'What is God?' and 'where did you come from?'

And then they start to lose their elder relations they are told they are in heaven, they have gone to heaven.

Another word that man has created to describe what you call the afterlife.

And the child is satisfied until such time he questions again where is heaven? Where will I find heaven?

Must I wait until I join my grandparents; my parents?

And that question by and large is left unanswered.

Friends can you not begin to understand that if they were told the truth of the existence of a world beyond this physical life, would they not be comforted?

Would they not begin to understand that their life on earth is merely a short, learning experience?

They could be educated in the ways of peace, of brotherhood, good will to all men.

Told that if they help others they will be rewarded but not materially. They will be rewarded by helping their fellow men without expecting reward, but their reward shall be greater than you can imagine.

I have spoken many times of the people who struggle in their physical lives to gain materially. To hoard the wealth, only for their own self-interest in mind.

My friends, I need not tell you they are never, ever satisfied.

You will know of such people who continue to reap material rewards, merely for their own prestige, to maintain their own power, if that is what you call it.

When you look at such people, you will know that deep in their hearts and minds they are not experiencing harmony with others. They are not experiencing the love that is around them in abundance.

They are not absorbing the love that is all they need, and as a result, you will find that their physical wellbeing is not as it should be.

I ask you to think of those you know, who you can compare with my words, and now think of those you have known who have been satisfied, who have given love, without reward, who have cared when care was needed, who have assisted those unable to help themselves, and have never, never considered the material consequences of their actions.

107

My friends it is state of mind.

It is a state of being that you either, have understood and nurtured, or you have denied; you have chosen a pathway of greed, material greed.

I again repeat, you will notice those who are pursuing a pathway of materialism are the ones who suffer the most for they are never satisfied.

They continue to experience problems, experience difficulties in progressing in the way that they have set themselves.

They never consider those whose lives they share. Never consider that if they were to share the material wealth not only for the benefit of those in need but to satisfy their own spiritual need, their own mental desires, their own spiritual rewards, their lives would be enriched beyond that which they aspire to.

Richness of the Spirit, the growth of the Spirit, the compassion that will develop within will be rewarded many, many times over.

But while they pursue a materialistic goal, an unachievable goal, because they are never satisfied, it will be detrimental to their progress.

And now may I compare an individual to a country?

There are many, many in your world suffering from homelessness and hunger; suffering from warfare. Children are orphaned, parents, adults are suffering because of the harm experienced in their surroundings and in many parts of your world there are people who have all their needs satisfied by their wealth and yet they want more.

They have more but they do not use it for the benefit of anyone but themselves.

I have spoken of this before. Are you not aware that the world's resources are plentiful provided by the great creator, your God, the Great Spirit, creator of all that exists, has created enough for all the people in your world?

Enough to feed everybody, enough resources to allow mankind to survive physically, and yet the situation exists that I have just described.

This situation is such that it generates disharmony, jealousy, anger, and my friends, strife and warfare because those who have so little feel that they are entitled to share the things that are available and when they are made aware of the abundance of food, minerals, so many things they are not allowed to share, my friends, are you surprised that they in turn will rebel against those who have?

We attempt to influence those who rule your nations. We attempt to break down their mental barriers, their attitudes towards the sharing of the wealth and the food and minerals.

108

We attempt to encourage them to open their eyes, open their minds and allow those who have not, an opportunity to share with those who have.

Friends, may I suggest that in some ways we are successful. It is at the expense of many lives being lost when resistance is felt.

Friends, I am one. One individual who brings you observations from our world to yours and there are many, many more on my side of life, yearning to encourage those who will listen, to abandon their ever increasing desires for that which cannot be achieved.

The closer they become to that which they desire, the further away it appears, but as I suggested to you, if mankind were to love one another, to show compassion to one another, to share with one another, that which they seek is instantly available.

For there is love in abundance, compassion in abundance, and those two words can lead to the peace that you all desire, and as I began, it begins with individuals.

It began with an individual, the attitude of mankind has progressed to the attitude of governments.

Meanwhile may I suggest you are privileged to experience my words. You by your presence within this building; have shown an interest in the reality of the existence of the world of Spirit.

But some, some I am sure were hesitant before you arrived. Some I am sure were doubtful that you experienced the voice of a man suggesting that he is from the world of Spirit.

My friends I ask you to believe what you hear. Believe what you see, and then on that understanding, your lives can progress in a more passionate and caring way.

We can suggest ways in which you can improve your environment, your lives and by improving your lives you can improve the lives of others.

Now, can you not see that as one does to another, each person can benefit yet another?

Individual progress my friends, progress.

The institutions that exist in your world are struggling to maintain their power.

They struggle because their motive is wrong.

They struggle to achieve that which is not achievable and my friends how many are able to see the error of their ways?

They suggest that the errors are not theirs, they are the victims of circumstance.

109

Therefore they try once again to do that which has failed many times before.

They are unable to see the realities of their failings and as such they are eventually about to fail.

Their lives, their institutions will begin to crumble under pressure of those who see the errors of their ways, who see the errors are repeated to the detriment of those who need a better way of life, a better understanding of that which is good for the fellow man.

And those who lead the institutions will eventually fall from grace.

They will fall from positions of power and, my friends unless they begin to understand the reasons for their failure they will continue to fall ever further.

That empowers me to speak of their lives to come, in the world of Spirit.

I have often been aware of people who have spoken to my friend Alan, asking him to explain the existence of the world of Spirit. Asking if there are people who reside in the world of Spirit, 'What do they do?' 'What do they do?'

There are many, many answers to that question.

There are those having experienced failure materially, have been unable to understand the benefits of giving without reward who are in need of education, in need of learning the errors of their ways.

For they will continue to exist mentally, spiritually, emotionally.

They still have their consciousness, their understanding, and through their own understanding they will become aware of that which they did in your world.

They will see where they might have helped when they looked the other way, and they will learn from those who share their existence in the world of Spirit until such time that they can progress to the next plane of existence, and that plane of existence allows them an opportunity to compensate for their wrong doings, for their misunderstandings of what their material lives were for and they in turn will enlighten others as they pass from one life to the next.

My friends you will all be aware of what you call death.

There are many confused people entering the world of Spirit.

Those indoctrinated by their religions, never understanding that they will progress and continue to exist into another life. They were led to believe there was heaven, paradise, even a hell.

When they become aware of their Spirit and in turn are confused, and they need the compassion, with a cry for love to help them to deal with their new existence, and then even more people are there to help others.

My friends, you also are aware of the people who pass to our world in a state of fear.

110

In a state of fear, in a state of unknowing, the groups of people who die together and pass to the world of Spirit, utterly confused, believing that they are still in their physical bodies.

They continue to roam mentally, in the world of Spirit, believing that they can still communicate with those they left behind, and they become confused because those people are unable to see them, are ignoring them.

Their mental state is in torture until they begin to realise that they have no physical bodies and at this time when we observe them in the world of Spirit, we are able to intercede, showing compassion and love to assist them in understanding that their lives will continue but not in a material world.

I have described just a few of the situations that exist for people who reside in the world of Spirit, striving to work for the common good and there are many, many more situations that exist to allow each individual to progress and learn and understand that life is more than a material existence.

I believe you speak of eternal progress?

My friends that is a fact. A fact of life.

Your progress is eternal.

I have spoken of my progress, yet I cannot begin to foresee where I shall be beyond my present position.

My progress will continue with Alan.

I shall continue to impress upon him the importance of sharing his knowledge with those who seek to know, and when his time arrives to leave the physical world then I shall progress further.

My task shall have been achieved; but I suggest that will not happen for many, many years.

Expressions of relief from Mollie and my wife, Pat.

There is much to do and we must nurture those who are helping to help others, with healing, knowledge, and understanding.

That is our mission and that is your mission.

I feel I must retire. I shall return. I shall speak with you once more. Allow me to retire. I feel there are others who wish to speak.

God bless you.

Our old cockney friend, Jack then introduced himself.

Jack: I'm Jack, you know what, I wanted to talk to him and ask him, I wanted to speak to you first, but he wouldn't let me!

Mollie: I should think not!

Jack: Don't he go on? I don't understand half the things he says. Not my type of bloke. He helps me but I couldn't spend any time with him; gawd blimey.

Mollie: I think he is trying to make you see the error of your ways.

Jack: What ways, the errors of my ways, no I'm just who I am.

Jack was asked if he'd found his wife Mary yet.

Jack: She came to see me 'cos I was asking, where my Mary was? And nobody would tell me, because I needed to think of her in a loving way. I wasn't thinking right, that's all. I wasn't thinking. They wouldn't let me go and see her because she wasn't 'in my area.' I didn't understand that.

The conversation continued about Jack's realisation that he had to think of Mary in order to communicate with her and that, as she had progressed to the next level, he wasn't able to just go and see her as and when he wanted.

He said that she was talking to him, but wasn't talking, 'if you know what I mean'. We just sort of communicated, like 'thinking.'

Jack: She's there, sometimes, but then she has to go again.

I've got to learn how to help people. If I help people, they will help me, and the more I help people, the more help I will get to see more of my Mary. I had someone to help me. I couldn't see him, he was just there.

He was making me think different. He was telling me I have to think love and think about my Mary so I did.

Thought I could see her and did not believe it.

Saw this light area in the distance. Anyway she was talking to me in her own sweet way, we don't talk, we were thinking. Anyway she was thinking things about me and I was thinking things about her, and it reminded us of what we used to think about one another.

Know what I mean?

Does that make sense?

Pat: You're progressing Jack.

Jack: Oh, that's a big word!

Pat: You're becoming a nicer person.

Jack: Didn't you think I was a nice person before then?

Pat: I think you were lovely but you just need to learn a few things about what goes on in the Spirit world, that's what Fine Feather tries to tell you, but you won't have it.

Jack: I can't understand what he's talking about half the time! Y'see what they do is, they get someone who I can understand. It's no good talking to me like he does, that's daft. I can't understand him!

Big words, meaningful things I don't know, so anyway that's what we do, alright?

I wish I'd known before.

Pat: Well it's taken a little time hasn't it?

Jack: I dunno what Mary did to disappear in the first place. Why didn't she wait for me? That's what I can't fathom out. Why don't she wait for me?

Jack was asked what he does in the Spirit world and he said he hangs around with his mates. He was told he wasn't getting anywhere, even though he said he was happy.

He was told that Mary wanted to progress further, that's why she progressed up to the next level without him.

Jack: Yeah, but when we were together, we did things together.

Pat: Yes, but Mary didn't go drinking with your mates, did she?

Jack: Oh no, no she wouldn't want to have been there. Anyway, my mates wouldn't have wanted her there either.

Jack was asked if there were pubs in the Spirit world and he replied indignantly, 'of course there are!'

Mollie: No wonder you're not moving on!

Jack: But we don't have as much as we want sometimes, sometimes things just disappear. You'll be enjoying it and then it just disappears, and I find I'm on my own again. So then you start thinking.

I start thinking about my Mary. Then while I'm thinking, suddenly there's Mary!

Pat: That's nice, so you've got to think more love, if you want to see more of Mary.

Jack: That's what I've been told – now you're telling me. Ok, ok, so what do I do if I want to go and be with her all the time?

Pat: You'll have to have a word with Fine Feather and see if he might have a little job for you to help you progress. Just see what he says.

Jack: I can't ask him, I can't understand him! You have a word.

Pat: Alright, we'll try.

Jack: Y'see, when he's here, and he's talking I can't get in, I just can't get in. He's just so powerful, gawd blimey. You just can't get close to him. It's like he's got this big light around him and you can't get into it. He's a bit important I think. I'm not scared of him he is so powerful that I just don't understand him.

You see I have energy, but when I come to see you, I haven't got the strength I had when I lived here.

Pat: It takes a lot of energy to come through, does it Jack?

Jack: I have to concentrate, that's the thing. 'Cos, I like it here. I've been here before, you know that. I like to talk to you. But, I'd like my Mary to come back and talk to you as well.

Pat: That would be nice.

Jack: Yeah but she can't, because I can't talk to her unless she talks to me.

Pat: Jack when you go back, just ask, if you can get through to Mary with a thought. Just think about her and it'll come, I'm sure. Do you agree?

Jack: No..........

Pat: You have to accept it. Last time you were here you didn't want to know it. You didn't want to progress.

Jack: What's this progress stuff? I'm here aren't I? Why do I want to do anything else? Why do I want to be anything other than what I am?

Pat: Well, you're just meant to go back and say that you want to see more of Mary, and then they'll give you the answer on what you have to do.

Jack: She's moved on and she doesn't want to invite me anymore. Do you want to meet Mary?

Pat/Mollie: Yes, that'll be nice.

Jack: I'll have to talk to her, when I see her. I'll keep thinking of Mary. See, I like what I do and I like who I am, what I don't like is when it stops all of a sudden! I enjoy it and then it's like, it's not there anymore.

Mollie: Well what happens then?

Jack: It's like I can't stay where I want to be. I feel like I'm on my own again. I had somebody with me when I came and I wanted to get him to talk to you, but suddenly he's gone.

Pat: Maybe he's waiting for you to stand back, Jack.

Jack: What would I want to do that for then?

Mollie: Well you're both trying to speak through the same body and you can't both do that at the same time, unless another one of us goes into trance.

Pat: It's a bit difficult for us Jack because we're not in the Spirit world.

Jack: It's difficult for me too, 'cos I'm not in your world, am I?

Pat: Well why don't you, sort of – I'm not telling you to go but.........

Jack: Yes you are!!

Mollie: Jack, Alan's only got one body so if someone else wants to speak you have to go.

Jack: Alan's body? I don't even understand where I am. If I haven't got a body, how can I live?

Pat: It's energy Jack. It's energy.

Jack: Energy?

Mollie: You're using Alan's body to talk…

Jack: So where's he gone?

Mollie: Where's he gone? I don't know, you tell me.

Jack: So you're saying his body's here, and I'm in it. I don't understand that. So I've got to go to let someone else in?

Mollie: I expect Fine Feather will be back soon, can you see him?

Jack: I can't see him, you feel him before you see him! Anyway, I'd better go. Nice talking to you.

Mollie/Pat: Nice to see you again Jack, thanks for coming.

Pat – (for the benefit of those who hadn't experienced this before) – Jack's not very well educated, he was a docker.

Another person then tried to communicate, with difficulty. The energy was dropping and he was confused.

He told us he had been a judge in Victorian times, and was now having to compensate for some harsh decisions he had made in sentencing some people in his court for minor crimes.

He realised that he was being allowed to temporarily inhabit Alan's body to speak to us tonight.

The purpose of his talk appeared to suggest he was experiencing the sixth Principle of Spiritualism – Compensation and Retribution Hereafter for all Good and Evil Things done on Earth. He was now being able to do some good things to help people in the Spirit world, and still had a lot to learn. He then left as the energy was fading.

Fine Feather then returned to sum up and close the evening.

It is your light that you shine upon the Spirit world, for some there is only darkness, for some there is little progress until the light of your love attracts them and then they become enlightened.

Your friend, Jack - very, very difficult to understand.

115

I attempt to enlighten him, to encourage him, but he is a difficult character, but we shall continue to tempt him to progress beyond his existence. It will happen but he has difficulties.

Your friend Jack is a good man, a very, very caring man and that is how we will appeal to his consciousness.

It is difficult for me to continue to speak for I have exhausted my intended conversation.

However it is my privilege to speak to anybody who wishes to speak to me.

If you wish to ask me a question...

Question – During 2012 has there been a change in consciousness?

Fine Feather: A change in consciousness? In 2012.............your year?

Yes.

There is continuous change. Unfortunately, unfortunately much change is not for the better.

However the change of which you speak is improving circumstances in your world. The understanding is such that when those who witness the suffering of others, they become more caring and compassionate and they are able to impress their feelings on others and therefore the progress that we seek, as I spoke this evening, the progress is beginning to reveal itself among the people who care.

It is very, very gradual, this progress. You inhabit a world in which communication is enhanced. Your communication is enhanced by the better understanding of your scientists to create things allowing you to witness the harm, the fear, the pain the suffering of many, many people.

Yet despite my words there is a very, very positive human condition called compassion of the mind and as more and more people become aware of the suffering that exists in your world, there is hope that those conditions will be eradicated for the benefit of all.

Those conditions did not become apparent only in one year, it is a progressive situation.

My friends I feel it is accelerating and that is for the good of all.

Our task, and the task of others is to enlighten individuals to the benefits they can bring by caring and loving and thinking positively that they can help those less fortunate than themselves.

Much to do.

I will try one more ...

No more questions were put forward.

Fine Feather: My wish is for the healing within this church will benefit all who enter.   My wish is that you present tonight, who have heard my words will consider that you have a responsibility to enlighten others to that which you have heard.   If you choose to disguise the source of your words then that is for you to decide, for there are many closed minds with whom you will need to communicate.

Therefore it may be of benefit to you to suggest that you, yourself have changed your attitude to your own physical progress, and that you will lead a less material existence and a more caring and spiritual existence.

My friends my words; your words, will be very beneficial to those who hear them.

I'm very grateful to have been permitted to communicate with you once again but I feel my friend Alan requires some respite from this communication.

Blessings from the Great Spirit to you and to those who are suffering, and I ask you to continue to show your compassion to enlighten others to the truths of the Spirit world.

God bless you.

Request for Help - 8 October 2013
Coulsdon, Surrey

In August 2013 a lady visited our church and introduced herself as Sue.

She told us that in her flat in Coulsdon, Surrey she was experiencing things that she considered were caused by a Spirit entity and, although she wasn't fearful of them, she found it a bit unnerving, as did her two young teenage sons.

Occasional unexplained noises could be heard and objects would move.

The hall light would suddenly be switched on and the sound of the dimmer switch could be heard as it was pressed.

In her kitchen a teaspoon had been left on the worktop and was later found in the spout of her kettle. Also, some pound coins which again had been left on her kitchen worktop were found standing on their milled edge, again without any logical explanation.

Sue started to attend our Sunday morning services regularly and enjoyed being in the church, but eventually she asked if we could visit her flat to see if there was anything we could do to help.

It was October before Mollie, Pat and I could find a suitable day to visit due to various commitments but when we finally got to Sue's flat on the morning of 8th October, Sue updated us on what had been going on in her flat, including her sons' experiences of hearing light tapping noises at odd times.

Her sons' shared a bedroom which had a desk, computer, the usual cuddly toys and other toys and games one would usually associate with teenage boys. They also shared a bunk bed.

As much of the activity was occurring in the boy's bedroom and we had discounted the possibility of the boys creating some of the activity, we decided to sit in the quiet of the bedroom to find out who, if anyone was causing the activity from the Spirit world.

Sue remained in her living room.

The curtains were drawn to reduce the light and, as usual, Mollie said a short prayer asking our Spirit guides to draw close to us and help us in our work.

It was often felt that whenever we did this work, we should expect a troublesome Spirit and perhaps, an aggressive individual, causing me to have to go into a fairly deep trance to enable the 'team' of me, Pat and Mollie working with our Spirit guides to deal with the problem.

I slowly became subdued and after a short time, while in a lighter state of trance than was usual, became aware of a presence with me that was in no way aggressive or unnerving to me.

However, I still felt a reluctance to allow him to speak through me, so in my mind I asked that Fine Feather draw close and perhaps, enlighten us to who was with me.

He gradually drew close to me with his familiar deep and reassuring voice and asked that we allow the man to speak, and that there was also a young girl who had been 'oppressed' while in the physical body.

So Fine Feather withdrew and a man began to make his presence felt.

Prompted by Pat and Mollie to speak he introduced himself in a very pleasant voice as Paul.

Paul had a south London accent and explained that he had lived in the flat a long time ago after leaving his parent's home.

After he passed over he realised that he had to progress into the Spirit world, but was prevented from doing so because he had become aware of a young girl close by who was very scared and unable to 'move on'.

Paul felt sorry for her and decided to try to help her but with little success. He told us her name was Angela and that she had been in a shelter during the second world war which had been destroyed by a bomb.

Angela's parents, among others were killed instantly but she had survived.

However, because the shelter was buried in rubble she had been left to die a slow death in the darkness, comforted only by her teddy bear, which she clung to for comfort.

Paul told us that he knew that he had to make his own progress but that he had to overcome Angela's fear and encourage her to move on into the light before he could move on himself.

Because he'd found himself unable to do it alone he'd decided to try to attract attention to himself by causing some of the phenomena that Sue and her sons had been experiencing.

He explained that Angela was also causing the type of phenomena that was generating fear rather than curiosity (as Paul was doing), explaining that as Angela was experiencing fear she thought it was normal and that to create an atmosphere of fear was nothing out of the ordinary.

The result was Sue's request for help, which was Paul's intention from the start.

So we continued our conversation with Paul during which he told us that he used to visit a 'pub down the road' where he got on well with the barmaid who used to top up his drinks for no extra charge.

There was little else for him to tell us, except that he knew of the two boys, the eldest of which was very intelligent and studious while the younger one was more mischievous and less studious than his brother, although he would turn out alright. (Sue later confirmed this was the case).

Paul appeared to be an easy going man whose sole purpose was to help Angela move on to be reunited with her parents, before he too moved on into the light.

So between us we tried to create an atmosphere of love and light to encourage Angela to trust us and come out of the darkness she had created for herself.

This was easier than we had expected because I felt that she trusted Paul and, with a little help from us three generating a lighter atmosphere, he was able to coax her to move towards a faint light that was beginning to show itself to her.

Paul was saying to Angela, through me, 'come on girl, look for your mum and dad, they're here waiting for you'.

As he continued speaking in a gentle manner, I saw Angela slowly emerge with her teddy bear clutched tightly under her arm, and move ever closer to the light.

An arm gradually appeared from the light and took Angela's hand as she slowly disappeared, but not before she turned and waved to Paul, prompting Paul to say, 'careful girl, don't drop your teddy!'

Paul then turned and thanked us, telling us that he was aware of a separate light which was welcoming him to move forward into it, and that his parents were there waiting for him.

The emotion was quite strong as we bid him farewell and shared his obvious delight at having helped Angela and allowed himself to make the next step in his eternal progress.

After a few more minutes Fine Feather returned and thanked us for working with him again and complimented Paul for remaining with Angela until she could be helped.

Believing, as we do, in the Seven Principles of Spiritualism, we felt that the sixth principle, Compensation and Retribution hereafter for all Good and Evil Deeds done on Earth, would surely be relevant to Paul's progress for accepting his personal responsibility (fifth principle) to help Angela.

Trance Demonstration - November 2013
Croydon Spiritualist Church

Greetings, my name is Fine Feather. It is a wonderful experience for me to be enabled to communicate from my side of life to yours.

It is a rare opportunity for me in the world you call Spirit to make ourselves known to those who hesitate to accept our existence and our ability to communicate, and I suggest that it is our responsibility to enable those seeking the truth of the existence of their loved ones, however it is our responsibility to prove to you that we are here, willing to assist and willing to respond to your desires, your prayers, your thoughts.

It has been said many times, many, many times that your thoughts are living thoughts that influence the world in which you live.

They do much good but they are capable of bringing much harm, when undesirable thoughts are given out. You understand?

There is much love within the walls of this church, there is much love. Also there is much doubt, there is doubt.

Those sitting before you with open minds, with doubt and it is my humble intention to attempt to remove that doubt and ask that they in turn will enlighten those of their acquaintance who are unable or unwilling to be here this evening.

For there are those who witness, but there are others unable to witness who can be informed of that which they have witnessed.

It is your greatest responsibility to help others understand the truth, the purpose of what you call 'religion'.

These are barren ideas, they are barren of originality, and that the purpose of religion is to seek a better way for all mankind.

It is not to create dogma, it is not to create disharmony. It is not to force opinions of one onto others.

The purpose of religion is to worship the great creator of all things, of all peoples in awe of the achievements of the Great Spirit.

In awe of the capabilities that he has given us as individuals, the capabilities to draw on his love, his inspiration, his peace. To nurture that which he desires for the world for all peoples throughout your world. The purpose of religion.

And yet, as I have said many times, your religions are the cause of so much strife, disharmony, destruction, all for the purpose of supporting the powerful hierarchies that are ruling and ruining your lives.

It takes a great man to think openly to those who fight with all means to defend their beliefs and their power and in your history here have been such men, who have spoken about the light of God, the love of God, the love of your fellow men. The need for harmony, for sharing.

Their fate has been subdued. Sometimes incarcerated and sometimes put to death.

It is the way of your modern world such things are more rare than they once were, the primitive man of many, many centuries before do not exist in fear as they once did.

Primitive man is no more, they are able to speak to listen, to learn, to enable the centre to have a voice.

There are those who speak of harmony, peace and love and there are those who will listen, but my friends, there are many, many more who choose to ridicule your attempts to change the world.

Your attempts to enlighten troubled souls. To enlighten the hierarchies of your religions and your governments. But it is necessary to enable those of us who are able to speak through a medium who has dedicate much time to create the conditions through which we can speak.

This progress cannot be halted.

There are many, many such people in your world, but relatively few who will listen and take seriously the truths and the wisdom, and the light of guidance from the world of Spirit, to understand the purpose of life, the purpose of living your life, unselfish people living in harmony with one another, in harmony with nature and in harmony with the Great Spirit you call God.

My friends, although you are few, you are not a minority. The majority of people living in your world desire the peace and the harmony of which we speak. They desire opportunities to break free of the shackles and the bonds and the dogma of their societies. They seek a better way. They seek to destroy those who suppress them but find that they are forced to continue to live in the way that they have been told.

My friends that is not a desirable way.

Therefore it is important that my words are spread far and wide to those who have not listened but who are pretending to listen, and I, like so many others from my world will continue to speak of the love and the peace and the harmony that is available to all, but the majority choose to ignore.

My friends it is your responsibility to repeat what you have heard, to repeat what you have witnessed, to reflect on my words and decide for yourselves if I speak truths, if I speak from a position of power that I wish to enslave your thoughts.

If you depart this room after I have spoken, with such thoughts, that I choose to empower myself over you, my friends my mission has failed. I have no desire to impose my thoughts upon you, only to enlighten you to the possibility of a better way, working together through the love of the Great Spirit.

It was not always so.

The many, many religions of your world, there were those who lived in harmony, in peace, working with one another to create a more equitable life of peace and harmony.

Indeed, when I existed in your world we worked for our fellow man, and these were not just blood families. All families were groups of people working in friendship and harmony with the world of nature creating for each other that which improved the lives of all.

It was not only the region in which I lived but there were others that I knew not of during my life in your world, but I have become aware of since I entered the world of Spirit.

My friends, that which you call progress has tainted the way of life of so many people in so many places. That progress destroyed the societies that were nourished by nature, were nourished by the Great Spirit, that were nourished by the understanding that what you did to each other, what you did to nature, would return to influence your future lives and therefore they were at harmony with all around protecting rather than destroying.

Protecting rather than causing damage. Protecting for our future generations, creating conditions so they could enjoy the same environment that we enjoyed.

My friends, I have seen for myself that that is not apparent in your world.

I speak only of religion. Religion is a word. Unimportant, but it is a word.

Religion has been created to nurture the egos and the power of those who seek to lead you. My friends, true religion, true religion is service to your fellow man. Service to nature, service to all that God created in a nation which shall be protected for future generations.

I feel that my message is repeated each time I am privileged to speak. My mission is intended to encourage you to seek for yourselves a better way of living, and to encourage you to influence those who may be in positions of power but through their consciences, are not content with that which they do. They are not content to they see the harm, the death, the destruction caused by a strong adherence to dogma but their consciousness can be influenced when they speak to those who speak sense. They can encourage them to consider a better way, to encourage them to think beyond that which they have always been taught. Change the way they work with others. Not the way for privilege but for the benefit of all those within their field their area of influence.

There is a saying of which you speak, 'from an acorn a mighty oak can grow'. If more dedicated people would allow themselves to be enlightened to the truths of a further, continuous life beyond your physical life.

Why is it so difficult for people to understand?

They fear the unknown because it is unknown.

Why is it unknown?

Because they are not enlightened by those who know the truth. Those who are content to know the truth. Not empower themselves to promoting those who are seeking to know the truth. Knowledge is of no use unless it is spread to others.

Knowledge, not faith, not belief but knowledge.

You have it within yourselves to enlighten others to the truths of which I speak, but so many of you choose not to do so. That's because of the fear of ridicule. The fear of reaction from others.

That I understand.

But if individuals here, many people speak of that which they have witnessed, more individuals will become enlightened, more and more people will become informed of the truths of life after the physical departure from this earth.

For those who are unable to comprehend 'what is life without a body?'

Yes my friends, I hear the questions, share the conversations, and sometimes I influence the words that my medium speaks, often he has said, 'where did that come from?'

Words which he spoke were not of his natural speech. But they were the words that were sufficient to enlighten the person to whom he was speaking. To sow seeds to enable them to search and discover for themselves in their own way the truths of which we speak.

124

My friends we do speak the truth. For what would my purpose be if I were to visit you on these occasions and say words which make no sense that made you doubt, that made you question.

If you depart with a sense of being cheated by the individuals within this church, my friends if any of you feels that I am speaking anything other than the truth then I suggest that you should not have arrived today because your mind is closed to the possibility of communication between two states of consciousness.

Consciousness.

Without consciousness there cannot be life. Without consciousness nothing can exist. If I had no consciousness, I would be unaware of your existence. I would be unaware of the existence of anything.

And so with you.

When you depart this physical life, all that will remain is your consciousness, awareness, understanding, comprehension. You use your words.

I seek to use the words available to me and there are many.

Consciousness of your surroundings. Consciousness of your individuality. Consciousness of all that is, was and will be. That there is life after your physical life.

Better to communicate through consciousness.

Your thoughts continue to live, therefore your thoughts are very powerful. Wisely my friends, use them wisely.

Do not speak of harm to others. Do not speak badly of others. Those thoughts will surely return to influence your lives in the future.

Thoughts of love, peace and harmony, of healing as you speak, of healing they are used by us, in the world of Spirit to create harmony, peace and love throughout your world.

My friends it is often said that you call your religion a minority but look around you, beyond the shores of your region and look at the need of people who care not for religion. Eyes send out a question of why they are suffering when others are not.

Are they not seeking the power and love of the Great Spirit?

Do they not plead for more harmonious conditions?

Do you think they are not aware, that as they seek to find nourishment, water, that they are not aware that it is available to you in abundance. Of course they are aware!

Friends, were you suffering the conditions that they suffer, would you not feel the same?

Yet you are unable to associate yourselves with their suffering.

You are unable to create the conditions where you can share much more than you do to enable those without to become more nourished and at peace with themselves.

The conditions in your world create much disharmony, but so much more could be done to destroy the disharmony that exists.

So much more could be done to destroy the jealousy that is created by disharmony.

By creating jealousy, you create conflict between peoples.

Continuous fight by those without to enjoy more of those who have a bigger share.

I have spoken for a long time. May I ask, have none of you considered your part in creating conditions to create harmony in your world?

Understanding that by your influence upon those who wield the power that they can become aware of a better way of life.

Those who have the power are no different from those who have not.

They are merely individuals who have taken advantage of situations that have propelled them into positions of power.

But within them they have a conscience and it is by appealing to their conscience that their actions can be influenced for the better.

It is a very, very hard road for you all to travel but it is a road that must be travelled if you are to see an end to the suffering and strife and warfare. From hunger, homelessness and deprivation.

You have many words to describe that which I speak of. I have used the words you prefer.

I have seen your world.

I witness the desire among many but little action from those people.

Desires are not enough but they are somewhere from which to begin.

People's desires must be harnessed to enable people to be influenced for the better.

I am aware that there are others who wish to speak to you this evening.

I have been impressed to withdraw but I shall remain very close, for I shall not permit anybody who has not earned the desire to speak, to take my place.

There are others wishing to speak. Some who wish to renew an acquaintance and others who are seeking, even in their new lives in the world of Spirit, seeking the proof that they are able to progress beyond the influence of what you call the 'earth plane'.

126

They need to be assisted to accept that they are not a part of the physical world and who are seeking to progress all the way into the Spirit world.

With your help and the light of your world we can encourage them to blend with the light of those who have gone before.

I must withdraw. I feel that I have depleted my medium.

Bless you.

Mollie/Pat: God bless you Fine Feather.

After a few minutes of silence, as Fine Feather withdrew, another individual began to make himself known.

Spirit: They let me come back. (We now understood this to be Jack returning)

Mollie: They let you come back?

Jack: When I was last with you they told me go with her. She kept coming back to see me but I wasn't any different from what I was. But she was, I said, 'Mary why don't you stay here with me?' but she kept telling me she couldn't and I could not go with her so she went so I didn't know what to do. But you told me to look for the light and join my Mary.

He is so powerful. I feel he wants me to do something, but I don't know what he wants me to do!

He's a nice person but he keeps talking, I can't understand what he's talking about. I don't see him or feel him, he is around me. He has got all this light. He is so powerful. He is a nice person but he keeps talking and I do not know what he keeps on about. What's the point of him talking to me if I don't understand what he's saying?

Mollie: Do you tell him you do not understand what he says?

Jack: Well he must know.

I keep seeing all these lights, just light. But people keep disappearing. They're there, then they go! But I don't know where they go. I'm just me and I look out for you.

Pat to Mollie: Does Jack know he is dead?

Mollie to Pat: Well I should think so.

Mollie: You do know you have passed on to the Spirit world?

Jack: How do I get to the Spirit world...I don't know...

Mollie: You go towards the light.

Jack: What's that then?

Mollie: You go towards the light.

Jack: I know there's light...

Mollie: If you see anyone going towards the light then you need to go with them.

Jack: Why would I want to go towards the light?

Mollie: Because that's where Mary is. You want to go with Mary, right?

Jack: I told you that! My Mary..........she never used to leave me, you know. When we were together with our kids, she never used to leave me.

Mollie: I'll bet those three kids are there as well.

Jack: (is mumbling and very confused)

Mollie: What you want to do, Jack, is go towards the light. Go with all these lights you are seeing, you go with them.

Pat: Do you know that you've died?

Jack: Do I know where I died?

Pat: No, do you know that you've died?

Jack: Well I haven't died have I?

Pat: Well you haven't died but you've lost your physical body...do you know that?

Jack: I don't know. All I know is my boys, my Mary ...they've all gone...

Pat: Jack, can you see a light now?

Jack: The light?

Pat: Yes

Jack: I'm in light. Do you know what, that Fine Feather swamps me with light ...a sort of cloud... It makes me frightened of him. I don't like it.

Mollie: Do you tell him that?

Jack: I think he knows it. It's just that he doesn't talk to me like he does to you. I hear what he says to you but he hasn't said anything to you about going towards the light, why don't you go towards the light? He don't tell you to do that does he?

Mollie: That's because we've still got a physical body, so we can't go towards the light. You've lost your physical body...you know about dying don't you?

Jack: Well I know I'm not here ...you see this bloke here, he lets me use his body, somehow...lets me come in and...I become like I'm here again...

Mollie: You're just borrowing Alan's body at the moment...aren't you?

Jack: He don't stop bleeding shaking does he, either!

Mollie: What did he say.......!?

Pat: He don't stop bleeding shaking.

Jack: *I didn't shake like this when I was here!*

Mollie: You didn't shake?

Jack: *No...*

Mollie: Right, you've got to go towards the light.

Jack : *I can't go anywhere if I haven't got a body, like you keep telling me. Do I need a body?*

Pat: No you don't...

Mollie: You don't need a body.

Pat: Look Jack, when Mary comes to visit, as she goes away, go with her.

Jack: *She tells me that.*

Pat: Well go with her.

Jack: *I'm frightened.*

Pat: Don't be frightened, all your mates are there. Don't be frightened!

Mollie: All your mates are there, just take Mary's hand. You'd trust her if she were here wouldn't you?

If she came and said, 'come with me Jack', you would have gone with her wouldn't you?

Jack: *So I've got to...how do I move then. How do I move...?*

Pat: Just think about it. Just think that you're going to move on. You will!

Mollie: Just think, you're going to go with Mary, you love Mary don't you?

Jack: *I love Mary, yeah.*

Mollie: Need to be with her?

Jack: *Y'see, this Fine Feather, he's not...he don't help, does he?*

Mollie: He does.

Jack: *He's not helping me!*

Mollie: Well he's trying to.

Jack: *He keeps lecturing me, he does talk to me. It's like he overpowers me with his....with his words and thoughts, and I don't know what he's talking about!*

Mollie: I'll tell you what.

Jack: *What?*

Mollie: Let's forget Fine Feather. You do what we tell you. Do you see the light at the moment?

Jack: Oh yeah!

Mollie: Can you see the light?

Jack: I can see...

Mollie: Can you see the Mary? We'll see if we can get Mary here. Can you see Mary?

Jack: I can't see nothin' at the moment.

Mollie: You can see the light?

Jack: Well yeah there's always...

Mollie: Just go towards it.

Jack: How do I do that if I ain't got a body? You keep asking me to see the light.

Pat: Just think!

Mollie: Imagine it...it's a nice, loving feeling there.

Jack: Well yeah....

Mollie: Well go with it, go towards it. Go on let yourself go...

Jack: There she is. She's waiting there.

Pat: Oh she's there...

Jack: What have I gotta do?

Mollie: Well go towards it...

Jack: What, think...?

Pat: Think, yes.

Jack: But I won't go if I'm only thinking it, will I?

Pat: You will, you will...just trust her Jack.

Mollie: Trust. You can trust us. You've known us a long time.

Jack: Do you know what, she is really beautiful, that girl.

Pat: Well that's nice.

Mollie: She wants you there, she's missing you.

Pat: Go on.

Jack: Yeah...

Pat: She wants you desperately...

Mollie: Go towards her. She has got her arms open wide and she wants you there because she loves you.

Jack: *She...*

Mollie: Go towards her, go on.

Jack: *Can I come back again?*

Pat: You can come back and see us, yes.

Mollie: You can see us when you want to. Fine Feather will let you.

Jack: *Yeah but most people...*

Mollie: But you go and see Mary first. Go and see Mary...

Jack: *(gently) Oh, that's nice...*

Mollie: Nice, isn't it...?

Jack: *They are all there they are all waiting for me now. It's nice innit?*

Mollie: You can trust us.

Jack: *Oh, yeah...but I don't want to leave you lot.*

Mollie: Oh, you can come back and see us when you want to.

Jack: *Yeah...are you sure?*

Mollie: Any time, we'll be pleased to see you. You can tell us all about it then. You can tell us what you discover there.

Jack: *(appearing to be in awe of what he was seeing) Oh that's nice...*

It seems that Jack had now 'moved on' to the next phase of his existence.

Re-united with his beloved Mary, his 'kids' and his old mates.

There was once again a short period of silence before we had a visit from another person who had spoken to us before, Archibald, the pompous professor who had previously insisted that he had come to give a lecture.

Archibald: *(in a very pompous, arrogant voice) Who are you?*

Mollie: Who are you?

Archibald: *A question answered with a question – that's a woman.*

Pat: It's a woman, did you hear what he said, 'It's a woman'.

Archibald: *This building, it's a church?*

Pat: Yes it is.

Archibald: *This is where I came before, but you told me I could not give a lecture.*

Mollie: No...

Pat: We did…

Archibald: I always lecture as I wish.

Mollie: Not today, it's my church.

Archibald: This is not your church.

Mollie: This is my church.

Archibald: This is my lecture room.

Mollie: Oh no, no.

Archibald: This is my lecture hall, I choose to speak on science.

Mollie: What are you going to talk about?

Pat: Science.

Archibald: That is my subject. I lecture on science, but you…you forbid me from doing so!

Pat: You forbid him from doing so. It's Archibald isn't it?

Mollie: Is it Archibald?

Archibald: It is Archibald. Professor Archibald Roberts. Now, if you will depart I can continue with my lecture! This…please depart woman!

Mollie continues to remonstrate with the Professor.

Mollie: You can't….go on then, go ahead. What are you actually going to talk about?

Archibald: Can you not see there are many here waiting to hear what I have to say? They are here! They have pencils and paper, waiting to er…hear my words on the subject of science.

Mollie: May ask what your subject is tonight?

Archibald: Science, medicine, new discoveries. We are living in an exciting world of new discoveries. I am the foremost expert…..

Mollie: In what?

Archibald: The subjects I wish to speak on!

Mollie: I'm asking you what you want to speak about.

Pat: New discoveries.

Archibald: Did I not say that?

Pat: You did.

Archibald: I wish to speak on science and medicine…

Mollie: Go on then.

Archibald: ...and more importantly, recent developments, the progress of science. Science is progressive. It is progressive, and therefore it cannot stand still. We must inform those who wish to impart their knowledge. So they can experiment with the knowledge they have, so they can discover for themselves. I encourage a voyage of discovery and I encourage them to use the experiments I tell them of, to prove for themselves that which I teach. That is progress madam!

(Much amusement at the tone of the Professor's voice).

Pat: Professor, can I just say something?

Archibald: Can I stop you?! Do these people here wish to hear you or me? Do they wish to hear you or me?

Pat: You came once b'.... (interrupted)

Archibald: What knowledge do you have of sciences?

Pat: None.

Archibald: Therefore, depart! Please depart!

Pat: You came once before, do you remember?

Archibald: Yes, madam...

Pat: You remember.

Archibald: You were...erm... less than polite to me.

(Much laughter).

Archibald: ....as you are this evening

Pat: I called him Archie instead of Archibald

Archibald: Please depart!...I have my lecture to give, I have already lost some time because of your intercession.

Mollie: What is your subject tonight?

Archibald: I have spoken of my subject, the progress of science. The progress that has been made in the development.. New ways of thinking. New medicines. New...oh, why am I telling you this? Please depart.

Mollie: Because we are ignorant.

Archibald: You are not of any interest in this subject.

Pat: We're getting nowhere.

Mollie: What I want to know is, what is the latest medicine?

Archibald: Would you understand if I told you?

Mollie: I would.

Archibald: Would you understand the words, the science?

Mollie: I would.

Archibald: Would you understand them as I have? You have to progress gradually. You do not start at the top of the ladder. You must begin at the bottom and progress...

Mollie: I just want to know what the latest medicine is.

Archibald: We are experimenting with new bacterial remedies. Bacteria is not entirely a disadvantage. In some ways it is there for us to manipulate for the benefit and the cures of the many ailments that exist among the poor. You understand!?

Mollie: Yes, of course!

Archibald: Oh!!!

Mollie: Well I'm not daft.

Archibald: Well...er, that's your opinion!

Pat: (Laughs at the Professor's response).

Mollie: What did you say?

Archibald: Well...the word you used is not one I would have used. It is to do with intelligence and that is not a word related to daft. Intelligence is a gradual understanding of the procedures necessary to experiment and you begin with very, very basic experiments. As I said, you do not start at the top of the ladder, you begin at the bottom and you have missed many of my lectures because it is not one where women show any interest.

Mollie: So you don't have any women at your lectures?

Archibald: I have not said that. It is my opinion that the subjects of which I speak appeal to gentlemen of a certain distinction and ladies are more inclined to remain in their residences with their music and their sewing and er...what I might call mundane activities.

Pat: Where do you teach, Professor?

Archibald: I teach in London.

Pat: Whereabouts?

Archibald: I believe we have spoken of this.

Pat: Yes, we have.

Archibald: So why do you ask again?

Pat: (Laughs)

Mollie: Do you just lecture in one place or do you go around different places?

Archibald: I am resident at my University....but.....

Mollie: Which University?

Archibald: ...I am often asked to attend society gatherings to explain that which I teach to those who have an interest, such as these people before me. Now if you will allow me to progress. Please depart!

(Laughter)

Archibald: It is not my desire to speak to those who have not an interest in my subject.

Pat: Professor, can I just say something to you?

Archibald: Again?

Pat: If I were to say to you that you've died and come back and you're in the year 2013, what would you say to that?

Archibald: I could not use the words to a lady.

(Laughter)

Archibald: ...but I would ask you to reconsider your thoughts.   You are speaking of an impossible situation.   I am not dead and I have not come back from anywhere, because I have been nowhere, madam.

Pat: How do you spend your time then, lecturing in your University?

Archibald: That's what I do.

Pat: Right, ok.

Archibald: I study, I experiment.   Do you see madam, it does not end with teaching.   It continues with experimentation and each time we discover something new it enlightens the students to the possibilities. Their learning, their own progress, their own focus.   The excitement of discovery.   Do you understand my words?

Pat: Yes, I do.

Archibald: Oh! That's good.   Now, if you'll depart ...

Pat: (speaking to Mollie) Shall we ask him to see the light?

Mollie: Yes o.k.

Pat: I don't know. Can you just look around you....don't look at the people, but can you see a nice white light?

Archibald: If it is the subject of my discussion then I shall provide the light.

Pat: Well let's just say it's an experiment, that's it.

Mollie: Us ignorant ladies want to do an experiment

Pat: Just bear with us, ok. Can you see a light?

Archibald: I cannot see a light...I refuse to see a light...because madam you are making me angry. I choose not to see a light...therefore a light does not exist.

Pat: Oh blooming heck...!

Archibald: (now very angry) I am here to speak of progress in material science. Biology is the word I seek.

Mollie: Biology?

Archibald: (Condescending tone) You understand?

Mollie/Pat: Yes, we understand!

Archibald: (Condescending tone) You understand!!

Mollie: Yes I do!

Pat: Have you heard of Penicillin?

Mollie: What year is it?

Archibald: What year is what?

Mollie: Well what's the year?

Archibald: ...of?

Pat: Where we are now.

Archibald: ...my birth?

Pat: No, where we are now.

Archibald: It's erm...19...1925

Mollie: 1925!...

Archibald: Why do you ask? If I cannot enlighten you to science, I cannot even enlighten you to the date! ...madam you have asked me the date.

Mollie: Well, you see, it's very difficult to us because we're in 2013!

Archibald: Ha, ha, that is not possible. That is not possible. You see, there is only one existence, and it is 1925. I continue to lecture as I have always done. Those who choose to learn will benefit from my knowledge...

Mollie: Well, I think that...if you go...if you can see a light, and you're saying you don't choose to, you are just denying it but if you go towards that light, you will find a lot of people who are waiting to hear your lecture.

Pat: Yes, that's what I meant...

Archibald: They are here...

Pat: No, there's more where the light is.

Archibald: I choose...

Mollie: This is a church. You wouldn't lecture in a church, would you?

Archibald: That's why I choose not to lecture in churches.

Mollie: Well, this is a church!

Archibald: This is my lecture room!

Mollie: It is not I disagree with you!

Pat: Sssh... you'll make him angry.

Archibald: I cannot make you understand, why do you not depart madam?

Pat: Professor would you just...

Archibald: ...allow me to continue with my lecture. Is it too much to ask?...

Mollie: Well go on then, you give your lecture.

Pat: Before you start your lecture, can I just ask you to do one thing? Ok, and then we will depart. Can you please look around and if you see a light, go towards it, and that's the entrance to your lecture room...believe me.

Archibald: You are trying to do something that I am not able to comprehend.

Pat: Then, if I take it slowly with you...just look around...can you see a light? It may be very small. Can you see it?

Archibald: The darkness...

Pat: Keep looking.

Archibald: There is a darkness...

Pat: Ok, just keep looking. Don't worry about us.

Archibald: If there is a darkness madam, I cannot see.

Pat: Ok...

Archibald: Only darkness. What have you done madam?

Pat: I've done nothing, just trust me...

Archibald: I...

Pat: Trust me Professor...

Archibald: I am being pulled, why am I being pulled away?

Pat: Because your lecture is waiting beyond the light, your people are there. The lecture room...everybody.

Archibald: You have subdued the light, there is no light, it is darkness..........

Pat: Just go with what is happening. Ok, please trust me.

Archibald: I cannot see light. I choose to remove myself from here. There is no light. Perhaps on my return, you will allow me to give my lecture. I shall depart. You shall remain in your church. I shall continue to lecture.

With that, the Professor departed and after a few more minutes, Fine Feather returned.

After speaking briefly about the Professor, he began to give a message to a member of the congregation from a man he was aware of in Spirit.

Fine Feather: There is erm...tension here.

(Laughter)

Mollie: We've had a bit of a problem Fine Feather...with Professor Archibald.

Fine Feather: Ah...our man of science.

Mollie: He didn't want to go.

Fine Feather: He will not. It is for you to continue to speak to him, as all men of science become blinded with their subject, are unable to comprehend the existence of another world. Unable to change their way of thinking and therefore their reality comes ... they are living in their own reality which as you and I are aware, does not exist except in the consciousness and mind of the individual.

We have to help individuals who are unable to expand their thoughts, their awareness of that which surrounds them.

Mollie: Have we managed to move Jack on?

Fine Feather: Did you become aware that as he departed and before I returned, there was another individual...he wished to speak to his daughter, his name is Harry.

Mollie: Anybody here whose father was Harry?

Lady: Yes!

Fine Feather: But he was very, very shy.

Lady: Yes thank you Fine Feather.

Fine Feather: Because of your conversation he found it difficult to make me aware of him. He was very, very unassuming and very kind hearted...I feel his presence, I feel his manner. I see him as a man of similar build to my medium, a tall man.

He had a very, very young face despite being older. His hair having been lighter, become grey and receding. Also he is showing me a smoking implement.

Pat: A pipe. He smoked a pipe?

Lady: Yes.

Fine Feather: He had a moustache. He had much love for his family. He devoted his time to his family. I understand he had opportunities to do things for himself but his family was his life.

I believe he is showing me he had grandchildren very, very loving family in his thoughts. I wish I could encourage him to return, but he is very, very shy.

That was his nature he did not like to be the focus of attention, choosing quietly to go about his life. Prayers for a lady are being heard. Indeed he wishes to help and he responds to the prayers of those who love her. I cannot glean any more from him he is not to re-appear to you all.

Lady: Thank you for bringing him to us.

Fine Feather: My pleasure, thank you for being here.

Friends...action from a man in Spirit whom I am aware of but cannot see.

An illustration of the power of Spirit, and the love that they are still able to share, if only they are given the opportunity.

Unfortunately, there are many in your world who are, through their ignorance unable to witness what you have witnessed. It's a greater misfortune of those who wish to communicate from my side of life are unable to, because of that ignorance.

They shed tears of sorrow when they are unable to comfort a loved one, to enable them to know they are still close by.

My friends, with the greater knowledge that you have, you do your part when others become aware of their loved ones.

Feel the wonderful sense of peace and harmony within this room that was not there to me when I arrived.

Still there is much less fear than there was, and for that I am very grateful.

I feel I must depart but if I have not answered any of the questions that some of you may have, then I choose to remain a little longer.

Man: I was reading a book some weeks ago about souls planning things like the bombings. I found it very hard to believe that people on the other side plan to do such outrageous things.

I was just wondering what the um...well, do they plan things on Spirit side of life before they come to the earth plane?

Mollie: Oh I see! Like people come specifically to lead a life and to do things like that?

Man: Yes, to do things, like pre-ordained or call it what you like. I found it a bit hard to believe, you know. I'm just wondering what he's going to come up with.

Fine Feather: There is a very strong bond between individuals here in your world and to those in mine. The bond is one of love, and those who pass to the world of Spirit with a fear of what to expect are still drawn to the loved ones they have left behind, and they therefore find that they are unable to progress into what they call the unknown.

They are not in what is being described as a limbo land. They are in a world of consciousness but still unaware of the light of the world of Spirit. Is that what you find difficult to understand?

Mollie: I think you misheard what...

Man: It doesn't clearly answer what I said...

Mollie: I think Fine Feather misheard what you said...

Pat (to Man): Did you say bombs or bond?

Man: Bombs......yes. Terrible things are planned on the other side, that go on, on the earth plane and then they come here...

Pat: So you're saying that they're influenced in the world of spirit to make people down on the earth...

Man: Let's say, I'm on the other side – in the Spirit world, and I'm discussing with my, say, future wife that I'm going to put a bomb in a box. This is what I read in a spiritual book called 'Greater Souls' and I found it very hard to believe.

Pat: I've never heard of anything like it!

Man: I'm asking him, is it pre-ordained to do this on the other side?

Mollie: I wouldn't have thought so.

Man: It's hard to believe.

Mollie: Would people come over here, Fine Feather and have it already built into them to plant a bomb?

Fine Feather: It is not my experience. The influences that generate the personality of the individual are entirely of the physical world.

I am unaware of what you call 'evil Spirits'. Evil does not exist in a destructive form in the world of Spirit, but can be nurtured in a destructive form in the world of the physical.

It is very apparent that a child can be influenced by his parents, his friends and things that have upset him.

He will seek revenge and because of the structure of society he is not made to understand that as he behaves he will have done to himself.

He therefore progresses with a state of mind that can lead to a destructive physical life and therefore I suggest that that which I have spoken of; a better understanding of the love of God, the love of the fellow man, the harmony of the Spirit world, would help to suppress the evil that you witness in your world. Does that answer your question?

Mollie: Fine Feather obviously doesn't think that things are pre-ordained.

Man: No, I read it in a spiritual book. The author was saying that the medium was getting this from the other side and that they planned this and planned that, so it's obvious that you mustn't believe...

Mollie: Well obviously the Spirit world could have an influence here but I don't think it would be planned before the person came...

Man: Well that's what it was saying.

Fine Feather: I have to remind you that you are born with free will and therefore you make the choices of your life, but you are constantly influenced by those who love you.

The more you move away from their influence, the less they are able to help.

My friend, evil does not exist in my experience in the world of Spirit but I was very aware of the capabilities of man to create evil at the expense of the lives of others in this life.

Mollie: I think whatever information that author got, was wrong.

Fine Feather: I feel there are more questions than answers.

Pat: Robby?

Robby: Can I ask a question please Fine Feather?

Fine Feather: Please do!

Robby: My helpers and inspirers have been speaking for many years about a great change of vibration will be coming to the earth plane. Much chaos before the earth plane and the Spirit world can synchronise in the same vibration and things will be greatly changed.

Can you expand a little bit on that?

Fine Feather: I...same vibrations?...can you understand that all that exists is a form of vibrations? It is a word not properly understood in the context of Spirit existence.

However consciousness is the overriding creation. It is a word that describes life.

The vibrations of which you speak are simply a reaction to the love and the light that is generated by the thoughts between the two levels of existence.

Therefore, that which is the most powerful influence will seek to override that which is weaker. Therefore as I spoke, the more power there is focussed on the power of love and harmony, the greater its use on both sides of existence.

Therefore as you speak, you think, you desire, you pray, we react and use the energy that you generate but the more you do, we are able to do more still.

It is not as you would say...even...one for one.

You generate and we enhance and you will be aware that in many parts of your world there is a relative calm and peace and desire for peace.

It is smaller areas perhaps of ignorance, that suffer warfare, disharmony.

But are you not aware that around them there are many people who work to improve the relationships and the disharmony between peoples?

I feel your world is slowly becoming more peaceful, less likely to react in a dangerous way.

I hope that is at least in part, due to the efforts of us in the world of Spirit. But we need your energy, your desires your prayers, to enhance our efforts. Does that help?

Robby: Thank you very much, yes.

Mollie: I think we ought to stop now...

Fine Feather: All the energies are progressively depleting, therefore I am unable to continue.

I thank you for your presence and I trust you will heed my words.

Pat: We will.

Fine Feather: For knowledge is of no use unless it is shared.

God bless you.

ALL: God bless you, Fine Feather.

Strange Activity - Late 2013

South Norwood

During the latter part of 2013 a married couple named John and Sylvia left a message on the church answer phone asking for help with a problem Sylvia was having in their flat in South Norwood.

We asked them to come to the church during a healing service to discuss the problem and to offer some advice.

This they did and told us that Sylvia was seeing people at the back of their garden and also in the windows of the house opposite. They tended to just stare at her and, on some occasions there would be many of them apparently dancing around in the garden.

Sylvia would also see shadowy movement through the net curtains at her windows as well as other odd things.

We suggested that they come for Spiritual healing regularly, hoping to be able to solve their problem without having to visit their house, which they did.

They both remarked how nice the healing was and how they felt more relaxed.

However by January 2014 Sylvia was experiencing more problems and felt very insecure when John wasn't at home, so we decided to pay them a visit to see what we could do to help.

Mollie, Pat and I visited them on Tuesday 14th January at 10.30 in the morning and, after a short conversation and a look around their flat, we asked John and Sylvia to leave us alone in their kitchen/dining room while we sat together in a small circle.

Mollie started with a prayer for guidance and protection.

As usual after only five minutes or so, I began to experience 'feelings'.

I felt as if a band of pressure was being applied around my forehead followed by intense pain on the front left side of my head. I told Mollie and Pat what I was experiencing as I was not yet in a state of trance, just so that they were aware of what was going on.

It was obvious that there was someone with me who was making me experience their pain prior to their passing.

As I then allowed myself to become entranced I felt I was being influenced by a young man with painful injuries to his head and other parts of his body.

What followed was quite remarkable, in that it was so different from previous experiences we'd had, and certainly didn't match any preconceived ideas of what had been going on, that we had previously discussed among ourselves.

He began to speak through me and told us that he had been a young soldier in the Crimean War and had been badly wounded in the head during a battle.

He had survived long enough to be brought home to England in the hope that his wounds would heal and he would become well again, but with the insanitary conditions of the times and little understanding of the nature of infection, he had slipped into a deep coma.

Believing him to be dead, the soldier was then buried while still alive but told us that it hadn't taken him long to die under those conditions.

Over time (we can only speculate how long), he became aware of shadowy movements behind what he described as a dark veil.

(It was showing itself to me as a light brown net curtain through which I could see movement).

I have to explain that when I am in a state of trance and under the influence of a person in the Spirit world, I see things as though I am seeing through their eyes.

He began to realise that there must be something else other than his existence in the place in which he had found himself (which he described as a state of purgatory), but could find no way of moving across this veil.

However he somehow managed to show himself to Sylvia in a shadowy form similar to what I was now experiencing.

(By this time it was fairly obvious that Sylvia was a very sensitive lady and was able to see this shadowy world in which the soldier existed).

Knowing this, the soldier then began the process of 'making a nuisance of himself' in an effort to find a way to release himself from the existence he was experiencing.

The result was the chain of events that led John and Sylvia to seek help from our church.

Once Mollie and Pat started a conversation with the soldier, they were quite saddened by what he had told them and slowly suggested that they would be able to help him to make the final transition to the Spirit world, where he would be greeted by loved ones.

He had already told us that he had no memories of his parents and had not married so we assumed from that, that he was a very young man when he passed over.

As usual we suggested that he look for a light and to move towards it, but he could see nothing even though he was keen to follow our instructions to lead him away from his present environment.

Once again Pat and Mollie suggested he look for a light and as she spoke, a feint vertical opening appeared in the distance, but unlike previous situations we had dealt with, the vertical light gradually moved towards me and slowly opened like a curtain at a theatre.

The soldier remarked how lovely, warm and peaceful he was feeling as the light enveloped him and he felt a wonderful sense of love surrounding him.

He thanked us as he gradually left us but as he did so, I became aware of an even more remarkable scene.

It appeared that what might be described as 'the flood gates opening'.

I saw, as the veil of light opened, what seemed to be hundreds, if not thousands of beings 'flowing' through the light, away from the shadowy environment into this wonderful place of peace, love and warmth, and I knew that I had witnessed something very special.

Once again, the atmosphere became very emotional as we felt a huge wave of relief pouring forth, and we felt that we had enabled so many people to break free of their feeling of hopelessness.

Finally things became calm and I felt the presence of Fine Feather drawing close to me.

He said that he had been as in awe of what had taken place as we had and that what we had seen was a new experience for him as well as for us.

It seems that for various reasons, when some people pass away, they are unable or unwilling to leave the 'pull' of their earthly existence, possibly because of the fear of death instilled in them by their religion, or perhaps the ignorance of what Spiritualists call 'the continuous existence of the human soul' (our fourth principle).

Once again, as we spoke afterwards of what we had done, we felt quite humbled that we were indeed able to work in this way, and it appears that Fine Feather too had learned a lot from this experience.

And Finally

This has been a long, eventful and very rewarding journey for me.

Rewarding, not in the material sense but in the sense that I have gained a wonderful insight into what awaits us when we eventually 'die' or to use the preferred Spiritualist term, 'pass over.'

I have been very close to 'the light' and have felt its love begin to embrace me, almost to the point where I have wanted to go with the 'lost' souls who needed help to leave the physical world behind and go forward to a new life in the realms of the Spirit world.

I have been very privileged to have been introduced to my guide, Fine Feather and humbled that he should be using me to enlighten all those who will listen without prejudice and make up their own minds.

I make no apologies to the reader who expected to read stories of 'ghost hunting' and 'evil spirits' haunting people in a climate of fear. Such stories are for readers of fiction or perhaps, the programmes that are becoming increasingly common on cable television.

I firmly believe that when we leave this physical life having experienced so many things, good and bad, that have shaped our characters and made us the individuals we are, we take all those characteristics with us into the next life of consciousness and continue our journey into 'eternity' until such time that we blend with the infinite power that we call 'God' or the 'Great Spirit.'

Therefore my common sense does not allow me to accept what are called 'heaven' and 'hell'.

They are man-made illusions used to blackmail those who have been indoctrinated into believing in them and are unable to release themselves from the dogma of man-made religions.

The reality, I believe, is so different and I firmly believe that if mankind would only learn to exist in a spirit of love and understanding, putting into practice 'the Brotherhood of Man', the world would be so much different.

Greed would be replaced by compassion and wars would become unnecessary in a world where, to quote Fine Feather, 'nobody has too much and nobody has too little.'

I think it apt that I finish with those words from Fine Feather and leave you, the reader to draw your own conclusions.

Lightning Source UK Ltd.
Milton Keynes UK
UKOW02f0508051114

241080UK00003B/173/P